THE MINISTRY CALLED
FAMILY

DR. DAVID B. MILLS

KINGDOM RULE
PUBLISHING
WWW.KINGDOMRULE.COM
HAMPTON, VIRGINIA

A division of Consuming Fire Incorporated
WWW.CONSUMINGFIREINC.COM

Published by Kingdom Rule Publishing, a subsidiary of Consuming Fire Incorporated.

Kingdom Rule Nonfiction
Kingdom Rule Publishing

Kingdom Rule Publishing
206 W Taylor Ave, Hampton, VA 23663

Kingdom Rule Publishing is a subsidiary of Consuming Fire Incorporated
Visit our websites at www.consumingfireinc.com and www.kingdomrule.com.

Printed in the United States of America
First Kingdom Rule Publishing Printing: October 2008
ISBN: 1448611814

Cover design by Stephen Blackmon.

DEDICATION

This book is dedicated to my wife and children. Bernadette, thank you for your care, concern, companionship and yourchallenging me to be all I can be for Christ. Thank you for being both critic and cheerleader, always causing and aiding better choices and changes in my and our life. Thanks for your stand and character, letting me chase you since the second grade but not catch you until we both were committed to Christ and his commandments. I love you, appreciate you, and value you more today than ever. Thanks for being my best friend, and teaching me the Ministry Called Family.

To my children, Christian, Destiny, Miciah, Noa and Gabrielle I love each of you and am thankful to God as well as humbled to be your father. I want you all to know how proud I am of each one of you; both for who you are and what you mean to our family. Thank you for your love, laughter and faith in the Lord Jesus. Thank you for willingly making the sacrifi ces that come with having parents in ministry. It is through some of those sacrifi ces that you have allowed us to change so many lives for Christ. Th ank you for teaching me The Ministry Called Family.

To my MOM, Mary (Cookie) Mills, thank you. I am a lot of who I am because of your tireless and endless love and commitment as a parent. You have worked two jobs at times, but you never left me to myself. That was an example of your love. Thank you for your devotion, instruction and wisdom. Thanks for covering me, leading me, loving me, and correcting me. Without you I realize I would not be who God has made me. Thanks for teaching me The Ministry Called Family.

Jesus, never in my mind would I had even thought of living, loving and leading the life you have given me. Thank you for saving me, leading me, changing me. And even as I am still growing and learning all You desire in me and through me, I love you, I honor you, and I appreciate how you have taught me The Ministry Called Family.

To Bishop Steven Banks and Dr. Keira Banks thank you for Fathering and Mothering me and my wife and family spiritually, for without you and your instruction, wisdom I and my wife would not know this level of freedom and devotion and commitment to God's Holy covenant of marriage. Thanks for teaching us The Ministry Called Family.

TABLE OF CONTENTS

FOREWORD

The institution of marriage as the foundation of personal and social development has faced enormous warfare over the last several decades. The epidemic of divorces, co-habitation, broken relationships, children out-of-wedlock have exponentially increased the questioning of the validity of the need for marriage and family as we have known. Obviously, the fear of commitment has aided such alternative options that relinquish the bond and the fulfillment of a supportive familial structure. While fear may drive a person away from commitment, it is no doubt that the greatest source of happiness is found in a loving relationship – husband and wife, parent and child(ren), and brother and sister. It is the way God intended man and woman to find the ultimate joy of being in relationship together and raising another generation in love, commitment, and fulfillment.

Dr. David B. Mills proclaims this message in a masterful way that even a common person can understand and be equipped to battle the atrocious attack of the enemy with fierce boldness and tenacity. After all, the attack of the enemy to destroy the family is directly indicative of his plans to destroy God's greatest earthly blessing to mankind – the trusting dependent relationship of a family amongst each other. Pastor Mills skillfully argues that family is the hammer and chisel of our character and the greatest ministry of any individual begins within their family in which they are responsible to fulfill their unique calling according to their position and gifting.

The book is replete with biblical principles that will motivate you to commit to your spouse, commit to your children – and most importantly, commit yourself to raising a godly family. These pages will embark you on a new journey in which you will learn to admire and embrace God's greatest blessing for each husband and wife – the family and the ultimate joy and fulfillment it can bring. These pages will not only tell you what the Bible says about marriage, family and parenting but it will tell you the "how to's" of raising a great family!

His marriage is strong and thereby his writing here is validated and authentic. He has raised a strong family that loves each other and cares for each other. Therefore, this book does not just contain a message; it is his message birthed out of his experience and fueled by his calling and ministry. It will empower you to live a fulfilled and victorious family life!

Bishop Steven W. Banks

General Overseer
Living Waters International Alliance
Newport News, Virginia

PREFACE

When we talk about family, the reality for me is that it means ministry. It might not mean preaching, singing or shouting, but the mindset of living, serving, loving, yielding, planning for, and forgiving one another. Family is the incubator for our future. Family is the hammer and chisel of our character. Family is the place of seeding and planting our ways of thinking, believing and acting as well as reacting. The family is literally the training ground for our positive or negative future way of living.

God so believes in the family, that it's where he starts everybody. The family provides a place where we also get our traits and habits, both positive and negative. We get bad ones such as being shouters, worriers, doubters, even nose pickers, controllers as well as manipulators and procrastinators. Hopefully, we also learn some good ones, like praying, worshipping, forgiving, helping and supporting, leading and thinking as well as community building. We learn about sharing and caring in between the fighting, name calling and horseplay. In there somewhere we learn some keys of relating and serving. But most of all, the greatest thing we learn about is and always will be the continual choice of loving and being loved.

Whether our families are traditional or non-traditional, all families are always full of purpose. Having grown up in the projects and struggled with things such as a single parent home, the lack of a father in daily relationship, a season of drinking, drug experimentation as well as a plethora of other things, the one thing that brought some level of consistency and stability was my family. I had a single parent mother who wouldn't give up, shrink back, or expect anything but the best from us or for us. I had an older cousin that was like another mother. I had an uncle and aunt who were open to receive me and join in processing me from immaturity to maturity (for which I am eternally grateful and indebted for their unconditional love and support).

In addition to all that we were in church, doing ministry and leading in the church, there were times when I made the mistake of not making my own family my first priority. Thankfully God, and others who loved me, helped me rearrange my priorities to God's proper order. Within the family we will endure some of our greatest times of humility. It is within this family that we will see our own humanity, do true ministry, choose to walk and work in unity with one another. It is within this family that we have one of our greatest opportunities to see God's glory.

The truth is there are no perfect families because there are no perfect people. But in God's sight, yours is the one that was and is perfect for you. He knew the one we would be a part of and needed even before creation began.

Then the word of the LORD came unto me, saying, Before I formed thee in the belly I knew thee; and before thou camest forth out of the womb I sanctified thee, and I ordained thee a prophet unto the nations.

Jeremiah 1:4-5

Our hope and prayer is that through this book, God and His Word will impart to us all instruction and direction that will lead us back to the Father's intention. We all have been called to this ministry we know as family. We all need to remember to correctly prioritize our family as it pertains to doing ministry. It's time we as men, women and children of God answer the call!

One that ruleth well his own house, having his children in subjection with all gravity;

(For if a man know not how to rule his own house, how shall he take care of the church of God?).

I Timothy 3:4-5

INTRODUCTION

Our world has changed vastly from the days of the "traditional family" such as Ossie and Harriet or even Clair and Heathcliff Huxtable.. The reality of any family being traditional is in and of itself a false concept, because every family is made up of very different people.

The current divorce rate suggests that 50% of all marriages fail. Along with that it records the rising prominence of the stated reason being, what they term as, "irreconcilable differences". The "newfound" understanding of differences shouldn't be surprising at all when in fact all of us are different and come with inherent "differences". All of us knew that when we got married. Sadly, that word has sometimes become a blanket statement for something closer to selfishness and self centeredness; something we're all more than capable of.

And he said, Who told thee that thou wast naked? Hast thou eaten of the tree, whereof I commanded thee that thou shouldest not eat?

And the man said, The woman whom thou gavest to be with me, she gave me of the tree, and I did eat.

And the LORD God said unto the woman, What is this that thou hast done? And the woman said, The serpent beguiled me, and I did eat.

Genesis 3:11-13

The intention and motivation of the serpent in the garden is the same as that of our true enemy today. It has not and will not ever change. Our enemy's goal is destruction of the family by division and sin. The family is the foundation for all that God has ordained. He knows the family is the key to strong ministries and healthy communities as well as the avenue for God to show His glory.

Behold, I and the children whom the LORD hath given me are for signs and for wonders in Israel from the LORD of hosts, which dwelleth in mount Zion.

Isaiah 8:18

This spiritual war of intent creates the exploding reality we see today of broken and single-parent families. It creates the difficulty the blended family encounters while fighting for some form or ideal of unity.

The issue is not necessarily the amount of money we make, nor the history of our family. It is not one's affluence or the influence of one's status educationally or socially. However the issue is what one gives, how one loves; how one relates to another within our family that produces a healthy or unhealthy legacy.

There are no families that operate exactly the same in method, mindset or motives due to the fact that all people are different. We each have our own personalities, perceptions and past experiences which affect and form our views and perspectives. That said, all can and do have something to contribute both in wisdom and direction.

It has been said that families don't come with a handbook, but I beg to differ. Within the Bible we find an awesome blue print for the family and family interaction; we see the principles that lead to becoming the spiritual and biblical family that God has created us to be. Where there is a creation, there is always a creator and that creator's intention. With this intention we will find the creator's instructions. The challenge may be that like children we all believe we have a better idea than the one in authority. So we reject his or her plan only to waste money, time and energy and go through needless pain and numerous sufferings before returning to the creator's instruction.

The book you now hold in your hands is intended to help us to better understand and more clearly see that blueprint which the creator has given. I have found that every time a man or woman returns to the instruction manual (be that for a TV remote, bike, driving directions, etc.) his or her chances for success and completion of his or her chosen mission are significantly increased.

One that ruleth well his own house, having his children in subjection with all gravity.

I Timothy 3:4

God distinctively shows us in scripture how highly He regards family. He shows that family is His priority even before what we normally deem as ministry. Scripture explains that His true desire is that we would care for, give time to, and manage our own house correctly before attempting to care for, give time to or manage His house. The family calls everyone to serving, submitting and growing towards God and each other.

It is in the family that we learn limitations, rules and boundaries of respect and disrespect towards others as well as ourselves. Many of us remember when Grandma said, "Don't say another word!", "You went too far!", or Mama's "What did you say!" This is where we learned direction, through choices, good and bad, and through discipline and correction. Many a switch, belt, maybe even the extension cord (tell the truth and shame the devil!) helped shape, mold and make us into who we are; helped teach us how to survive in the world. One thing is for sure: the spanking brought forth immediate change in our thinking, our behavior and oh yes our walk! We also saw and experienced some submission, (hopefully not the step on, step past, step over type, but the get in step type) where as a child you learned that "You don't pay any bills here, so you don't control what we do here."

Within the family we learn some of our greatest lessons. By that I mean wisdom, usually from Mama or Big Mama, Grandmamma or maybe our Dad, that was beyond the level of who we were as young people. It was in the family where we learn right and wrong; our convictions of what we should and shouldn't do, what we should believe or refuse; how we relate to others, whether we tell the truth or whether we lie. In the family, traditions are passed down, such as vacation trips, family visits, holiday parties and things that were just good for the family. It's also in the family where we develop our perceptions, good and bad. We learn standards and values and some interesting thoughts and views. We pick up some stereotypes; sometimes racism, sexism, separatism, issues of judging and prejudging, usually based on someone else's mentality, history, education, experiences or sometimes even their personal injury. We learn different views of relationships. We see what they could be, are supposed to be and sometimes even what we definitely don't want them to be.

The reality is that in the family where we are supposed to discover our identity, find security, learn our history and be free to develop our own individuality. Here we should grow into a person who is mature; one who is physically and emotionally healthy. Here, in the family is where we are supposed to have a developmental safety net, so that no matter what we go through there is always someone that loves me and accepts me.

"To command is to serve, nothing more and nothing less"

~ *Andre Malraux*

CHAPTER ONE

THE MINISTRY OF THE LEADER (HUSBAND)

When it comes to the function and responsibilities that accompany the various roles of men, faulty definitions (from television, what I call "street instructions" and bad relationships) abound. Society has done their share to display the man's role as a stumbling, bumbling, emotionally immature, relationally challenged and irresponsible buffoon. All too often they are either being left out or laughed out of the true storyline. But thanks be to God that it is not up to men to define manhood, and not up to society to define God's intended leader in male authority as it pertains to the family and their destiny. The story does not end there.

I myself, come from a family without the stable presence of a father. As a child I spent time living in the projects. Drugs, gang violence and a high annual number of male homicides were harsh realities for me. I thank Jesus that I had the strength, faith and support of an incredibly strong mother, aid from uncles, and the encouragement of a host of other positive role models. I also had my share of failures, to help me make it through the process of personal growth (not that I have arrived, even now I am still a work in progress). Despite my meager beginnings, the grace of God has allowed me to not only survive but have a little success at becoming a Godly man, a loving husband and a growing Dad. That grace has also blessed me with the opportunity to Pastor one of the world's greatest churches (my thanks to the TTW family).

As men there are many things we understand and many things we don't. I think the test of manhood in the challenging of oneself to grow up; to grow out of irresponsibility, grow beyond the limitations surrounding you, grow beyond anything and everything others or even you believed you couldn't do. It constitutes an ongoing decision to be a man.

When I was a child, I spake as a child, I understood as a child, I thought as a child: but when I became a man, I put away childish things.

I Corinthians 13:11

That decision means there must be a shifting from childlike words, thoughts and actions, to manlike words, thoughts and actions. Boys like others to carry or take responsibility for them and their decisions, but men take responsibility for themselves personally, their families and their communities. We can really only develop into our leadership role after this shifting takes place and is displayed. Usually some difficulty or discipline begins bringing this to pass. There is never any growth where there aren't any changes, falls or failed circumstances.

To better understand this, let us look at manhood and leadership and how it applies to the following areas:

- Accountability
- Intimacy
- Humility
- Responsibility
- Spirituality
- Authority

There are more areas to manhood but these that we're going to highlight hold a great weight of priority and I believe these hold secrets to our victories.

LEADING THROUGH ACCOUNTABILITY

Why begin here? I chose accountability as our first principle because of its critical significance in our development. Men who are not accountable sometimes lose sight of or become distracted from the importance of our presence and purpose. Accountability brings a level of security, peace and assurance to our wives, and confidence to our children. We also find that only when we are accountable do we qualify for true authority. Rarely does anyone do something great without some level of accountability. Accountability is what makes responsibility a priority. Accountability is what makes intimacy possible. It is accountability that makes us mindful to walk in humility and it is that same accountability that causes us live right spiritually. It shows that we are able to be counted on, you bring all of your abilities to the problem, necessity or adversity happening within and to the family. It begins with headship, this is the one with the ability to lead utilizing all assets typical of the head. The ability of the mouth; to carry out communicative functions, the ability of the nose; to operate in discernment and wisdom for various circumstances and situations, the ability of the ears; having the maturity to listen to and for God's wisdom for the family, the ability of the eyes; the family is being driven by a God powered vision that it's leader must see, even the hair; a covering for protection and to keep from exposing that which may be lacking. God's goal for us is walking in headship, not creating headaches, and for our families to get ahead and stay ahead, far beyond the desires, schemes and plans of Satan.

For the husband is the head of the wife, even as Christ is the head of the church: and he is the saviour of the body.

Ephesians 5:23

It's supposed to be even as Christ or on the level of Christ. Our measuring stick is not other men on this planet, but being an example of the God of this planet. Even when we miss the mark, we have the shed blood of Jesus that graces us to get back on track. It's accountability that allows me to reign with God, even as Adam did with God in the garden of Eden before the fall.

And the Lord called Adam, and said unto him, Where art thou?

Genesis 2:9

Accountability starts individually (Adam), even though there was sin in the family (Eve). The call for accountability comes through the male initially, this is where we draw the reality that the responsibility for the condition of the entire family begins with the man in authority. It means if anyone in our family has a problem it becomes our problem. Headship is neither for the carnal, self consumed nor the uncommitted and is certainly not for the cowardly. Neither is it for the perfect, but you will, however, be perfected by it and the process that it entails. Accountability means answering the hard things, addressing the known things, inspecting the hidden things, and admitting the failed things. It means expecting those lives around us to be continually growing and changing while still keeping up with them. It's realizing that everyone around us is either assigned to us, connected to us, or has hopes for us, dreams tied to us, or faith for and towards us and at times dependence upon us.

Welcome to headship! Congratulations, and welcome to the reality of accountability and responsibility.

Let's take a quick accountability test. Do I discern the dangers in and around my family? Do I decide regularly and in a timely manner, or are they still waiting on me? Do I discover new things about the people, family, children or friends around you, independent of my own interests? Do I give them direction for or in our situations? Reality says that when there are directions given there are usually a lot less questions that need answering. As a leader how's my delegation? How do I demonstrate love? Who checks on me? Who asks me the questions no one else wants to ask me? See God has given us accountability not just for us personally, but for everyone under our authority. We're expected to be accountable for our location, our personal conditions and for every one of our relationships. You and I have been given the anointing, the calling, gifting and the grace to fulfill this call of accountability.

Now therefore fear the LORD, and serve him in sincerity and in truth: and put away the gods which your fathers served on the other side of the flood, and in Egypt; and serve ye the LORD.

Joshua 24:14

One question, Where are you? In God? With your wife? Your children? Where are you with the money, ministry and your family's God ordained destiny?

LEADING IN INTIMACY

Intimacy is the highest level of relationship. Intimacy is above what happens physically, verbally, and even what happens privately. The goal of intimacy is not closeness of proximity, nearness of person nor sameness of personality but oneness. The demand of intimacy is that we take the emphasis off of me or I. Let's address, before we go further, that by intimacy I don't mean sex, but the ability to know and be known by verbal and nonverbal communication, connection or expression from one person to another person. You may beg the question, so how do we lead in intimacy? We develop the loving leader within.

Live on her level, be an Ephesians husband, (Ephesians 5:25) one that dwells in the house. We're talking more than just being present and physically accounted for, but present and relevant in matters that are imperative for leading the family. What is it the home needs? What are her needs? What are the children's needs. How can I lead and properly take on my role in fulfilling them? Husband = House-Band We must be present in mind, body, will and emotions. We must have something input on decisions and it is necessary that we take the lead on the direction in which the family is going. After all, we have already learned that we are accountable for the outcome, have we not? Our example, our "exhibit A" if you will, is Jesus. He was willing to come into the house (natural world) and live around, among, with and for His bride (the church). Our task is much the same after having lived apart from, we have to learn to live around, in the vicinity and in availability to her and for her needs. We have to learn to live among our families. Jesus was capable of living in perception, reception and in connection, communication with His bride, and he lived for His bride. He lived in demonstration, submission, initiation, relation and as an expression of God's Love for her. In Christ's intimate love for her He was willing to enter her world and learn her ways, words, and walk. This requires a desire to lay down one's life, to give something. In other words a sacrificing to become one with someone. Leading is teaching, showing and living, as well as sharing an example, just as God leads us. He fully demonstrates His love for us now as He has in the past. So we must lead with the emotion, decisions, and actions that prove an intimate relationship with another person. We must love openly, unconditionally, and vulnerably, all the while with her and the family as your top priority.

Husbands, love your wives, even as Christ also loved the church, and gave himself for it.

Ephesians 5:25

It's a profound thing once you realize that the level of intimacy found in your family is up to you. The atmosphere will be as we create it. Is your atmosphere fearful? Is it fake or phony? Is it open so that issues can be dealt with or is it forced only dealing with things because we have to?

Then said Elkanah her husband to her, Hannah, why weepest thou? and why eatest thou not? and why is thy heart grieved? am not I better to thee than ten sons?

I Samuel 1:8

And they were both naked, the man and his wife, and were not ashamed.

Genesis 2:25

Intimacy is unashamed of faults, frailty, issues of our flesh or even our realest fears. For most men one of the highest hurdles is balancing "being real" and still being respected. Society gives us yet another false reality of what makes us real men; the tough guy, the thick-skinned guy, the one who walks around and feels no pain or shows no weakness. The truth of the matter is that the majority of us are operating from a place of not ever being free to openly relate our hearts to those we love and care about. The fact is that bound, inhibited boys will more than likely become bound, inhibited men. Told to be quiet, suck it up, but never told that it is okay to be open, to be real and communicate how you feel. That being said we have to take it upon ourselves to create an atmosphere that is conducive for this communication. Start with questions; ask her how she feels about the direction the family is taking. Find out what she thinks about. How was your day? How did the _____ on the job turn out? [Show her that you were listening when she talked to you before.] Then *be prepared to talk* and share your heart. This will require you to take time to truly reflect on your day and how you feel in preparation. Start your communication with the things you have in common.

Likewise, ye husbands, dwell with them according to knowledge, giving honour unto the wife, as unto the weaker vessel, and as being heirs together of the grace of life; that your prayers be not hindered.

I Peter 3:7

LEADING BY HUMILITY

Humility is one's ability to control oneself and one's authority in and over oneself verbally, emotionally, mentally and physically. Therefore humility is not a weakness, but a demonstration of power over oneself and one's own F.L.E.S.H. (Fleeing Lust, Emotions & Sinful Heart). It's our ability to submit oneself personally, conquer pride openly, operate in brokenness privately, be yielded spiritually and reverence God totally.

Submitting yourselves one to another in the fear of God.

Ephesians 5:21

Humility is submission in action. Visible by expressions and made an example through demonstration, humility is displayed in our service to those whom serve under us and in authority over us, by dying to self, by making positive changes for others and most of all by repenting before God. Again our greatest illustration is Jesus. The King of Glory came to serve as a newborn baby. Divinity came to us wrapped in humanity, and yielded first to a family. We see that Jesus was submitted to His parents.

And he went down with them, and came to Nazareth, and was subject unto them: but his mother kept all these sayings in her heart.

Luke 2:51

Later we see that Christ submits to John the Baptist in the ministry of baptism.

Then cometh Jesus from Galilee to Jordan unto John, to be baptized of him. But John forbad him, saying, I have need to be baptized of thee, and comest thou to me? And Jesus answering said unto him, Suffer [it to be so] now: for thus it becometh us to fulfil all righteousness. Then he suffered him.

Matthew 3:13-15

For our last example we see perhaps the greatest act of submission known to man as Christ submits Himself to those who beat His body and crucified Him on Calvary.

Therefore doth my Father love me, because I lay down my life, that I might take it again. <u>No man taketh it from me, but I lay it down of myself.</u> <u>I have power to lay it down, and I have power to take it again.</u> This commandment have I received of my Father.

John 10:17-18

Yet we, as Christians (followers of Christ) fight tooth and nail with walking in, living in and loving in humility. We see that He served in the house of His earthly parents for 30 years before ever serving in the house of God.

He riseth from supper, and laid aside his garments; and took a towel, and girded himself. After that he poureth water into a bason, and began to wash the disciples' feet, and to wipe [them] with the towel wherewith he was girded.

John 13:4-5

Humility esteems others as higher than oneself. Even in His death, Christ esteemed us and our opportunity to live on another level as higher than His own welfare and well-being..Humility is the greatest sign of maturity.

And whosoever would be first among you, shall be servant of all.

Mark 10:44

The process of maturation typically happens in stages. Maturity starts with me telling you what to do, then moves to me showing you what to do, consummating with me being an example of what do; helping you to do as I do. The greater level of authority you are granted, the greater level of humility that will be required.

but he that knew not, and did things worthy of stripes, shall be beaten with few stripes. And to whomsoever much is given, of him shall much be required: and to whom they commit much, of him will they ask the more.

Luke 12:48

Two of the most highly regarded people in the Bible lived the picture of humility for us. Moses and of course Jesus clearly demonstrate that being a great leader demands willingness to be a great server. In the practical sense, it may mean doing the dishes or washing a couple loads of laundry, maybe taking on the school taxi service for the week. Either way, we demonstrate through our level of service the level of love and humility that is Christ-like.

LEADING THROUGH INITIATIVE AND RESPONSIBILITY

The actuality of being a leader means realizing that whatever God releases to us He requires us to act responsibly for. When we receive and become willing to do what God expects, we become liable for whatever that assignment may entail, whether it be someone or something. We become responsible for our location, decisions, relationships, and conditions as well as for our actions and re-actions to situations and circumstances. Simply put, responsibility is the ability for us to respond to that which is happening currently with ourself, our family, vocationally, in our city and even in our country.

Being a leader also means that I have to answer to both those I lead as well as to those whom I follow, because in any event my actions and/or decisions affect their way of relating or living. As men we have to begin to stop living or reacting out of fear, thinking only of failure or ridicule if our decisions don't work out for the best. At worst we can repent for our error and pray for God's help and grace in getting over it and fixing it. Then the next time call or contact someone who has experience in the arena of that decision.

We can't be in authority and refuse responsibility. Note; if we won't personally ask for the help of God, the Lord of Glory, and/or someone He has assigned to us, then that becomes an opening for the enemy to eventually get the victory. Where there is no one taking responsibility there you normally find poverty, confusion, and lives that are downright crazy. Men, make the decision! No decision guarantees your family to be in the same place they were yesterday. No decision ensures us staying in the same position and condition and will only compound the frustration your family most likely already feels. Decide to decide. We all need someone in our lives we can pose questions to before we make decisions, a wife, friend, mature family member, maybe even a neighbor. Iron sharpens iron. Take an initiative that will cause things to happen, make some motion, that is what begins every journey to our destiny, someone has to take initiative.

The first sign of maturity is the ability to take personal responsibility for whatever, whoever, wherever, whenever. Not just take responsibility but take the initiative to communicate to and educate the family on what has been decided and the role they are to play. Responsibility is doing what we have to do in order to do what we want to do. Responsibility means meeting the needs of the people around me, to the best of my ability. Sometimes even before they ask me to. The responsible leader has an awareness of the condition and needs of others. It means knowing and doing what is necessary. Note this; responsibility doesn't always have an answer but is always looking for one, and plans on returning with one in a reasonable timeframe.

The mature, responsible leader has the answer or is searching for one. However, that mature responsible leader must also be able to demonstrate the maturity required to admit it when you don't have the answer.

And the LORD God took the man, and put him into the garden of Eden to dress it and to keep it.

Genesis 2:15

For the husband is the head of the wife, even as Christ is the head of the church: and he is the saviour of the body.

Ephesians 5:23

Therefore shall a man leave his father and his mother, and shall cleave unto his wife: and they shall be one flesh.

Genesis 2:24

And if it seem evil unto you to serve the LORD, choose you this day whom ye will serve; whether the gods which your fathers served that were on the other side of the flood, or the gods of the Amorites, in whose land ye dwell: but as for me and my house, we will serve the LORD.

Joshua 24:15

But God commendeth his love toward us, in that, while we were yet sinners, Christ died for us.

Romans 5:8

LEADING SPIRITUALLY

One of the challenges of manhood is defining when we become the leader. It is when we take the initiative, when we are willing to try to lead, when we choose to be out front, and when we are willing to take to responsibility for what happens now, next and in the future.

Leading in Prayer - When we talk about prayer some people immediately think of their inadequacies, and not of God's authority and ability. The truth is that God is waiting in expectation for us to call out to Him and talk to Him concerning every situation in our life. He says cast your cares on me. When someone cares for you, it means more than them taking a mere interest in you, but having an earnest desire to be involved intimately in all areas of your life, whether those areas are going well or they're going in a direction that is not so well. Prayer is communicating with the God the Father, Christ the Son

36

and the Holy Spirit instantaneously. He desires to hear our heart and to be trusted in answering the way in which desires. It takes faith to talk, as well as to wait on His answer. We don't have to know how to pray like a famous minister to be a spiritual leader, we just have to pray consistently and earnestly. There is no set time, way or place to pray. We can pray anywhere at anytime. Just start praying before you leave out together, before bedtime, before releasing the kids out of the car, first-thing when everyone gets home, thirty minutes prior to bed time or even while driving. Always ask your kids to pray as well, this will ensure that you get an idea of what's on everybody's heart within the family because they will pray about it. Listen for what God has to answer and for what you can answer as a husband, father or friend. In regards to praying for and with others, the best time to pray for someone is as soon as they ask. Don't wait until later because we all live busy lives and it can slip your mind before you know it.

Ask, and it shall be given you; seek, and ye shall find; knock, and   it shall be opened unto you.

Matthew 7:7

Leading in Worship - Leading in worship is more about example than anything else. If we prepare ourselves properly; time, clothes, schedule and food ahead of time we will demonstrate the importance of worship. One habit in our home is Saturday night. I iron and put out my clothes out as well as the kids clothes. They take their showers the night before and just wash up in the morning. This causes our family to take worship seriously, because it illustrates that it is important for us to prepare for the presence of God. It also shows God that we have a high expectation of meeting Him. You see it becomes like an

THE MINISTRY CALLED FAMILY

appointment in His presence. If you were going to meet the president you wouldn't stay out late, wake up and get ready any kind of way. How much more for the King of kings and Lord of lords.

Lead in Repentence - To be the leader is to be the leader when right and when wrong. It's being the first to admit the things done wrong. It must be admitted in the spirit first, because like Adam before me, I am responsible for the conditions and atmosphere in my home (not Eve). Whatever goes wrong becomes my burden and I must play a predominant role in correcting it. Understand this, as the head, I always bear the weight of answering to God for the state of my family, even though my wife does have a level of personal accountability. One of the best ways to operate in authority is by demonstrating humility in repentance before a holy God.

But he that is greatest among you shall be your servant.

Matthew 23:11

Leading in Living - You lead in living with your daily being and by walking out what God is doing in our life. The level of the family's spirituality, integrity and honesty is an indicator. Whether we will be holy or ugly will begin with me and my lifestyle. In other words, whatever level you want for your family has to become the level you decide to live on yourself. Your words become their words, your ways become their ways, and your walk becomes their walk. It's more than just being around them, our lives become a mirror and a measuring stick to them. In my house I have pronounced "what you do for one, you do for all", and ever since then I've had to pay the price ($$$literally$$$) for it. Remember, I have five children. Roughly translated that means 1 x whatever it is = 5 x whatever it is. That also regularly challenges me to not walk in favoritism with my children. Pray for me and for them!

Leading in Service - Serving also means leading the house in the day to day issues. At times that will mean in the cleaning, vacuuming, washing clothes and washing dishes. Don't always ask them to do it. I can do it myself.

Even as the Son of man came not to be ministered unto, but to minister, and to give his life a ransom for many.

Matthew 20:28

When it comes to cooking I didn't do this until as recently as three years ago because of a lack of faith. However, out of necessity (I asked Bern to return back to working) I grew in my culinary *skill*. That *skill* part is debatable depending on which of my children you talk to. You see men, I didn't marry my mother, I married my wife. I'm in her home just as much as she's in mine. I figure if Jesus can wash the disciples' feet I can wash my kids clothes, wash their dishes and clean the house. Oh, by the way, I live and eat there too.

THE HEART OF AUTHORITY

When we say authority many people think of the hardest, most rigid or most wounding things and/or people they've known in their lives. Truth is authority does not just pertain to how we work, but it also applies to our daily lives. You can't even come into this life or leave this life without somebody's help. Usually that somebody is someone in authority. When coming in we submit to the nurses and the doctors at the hospital. On the way out there will be six to eight other people's strength and authority that will carry us on to the place that the earth will receive our body. God has made it so that at every age and at every stage you and I will have to submit to someone's authority. From birth we submit to the authority in our families, then at day care we will submit to a provider's authority. When we access elementary, you guessed it, we have teachers we submit to. Next we go into middle school, there is always a principal, vice principal and teachers at every school. Then when we reach high school and we just know we are grown. Those adults, old heads and some grey heads are still there, holding that authority over us. Then the real world kicks in upon graduation and obtaining one's first working position, that with it, and every subsequent position comes someone in authority over us. The Bible speaks of authority and lets us know that nobody in authority got there without God's wisdom and sovereignty.

Let every soul be subject unto the higher powers. For there is no power but of God: the powers that be are ordained of God.

Romans 13:1

The real deal with authority is that as long as you don't violate it, minimize it, dishonor it or ignore it, you can and will be blessed by it.

Whosoever therefore resisteth the power, resisteth the ordinance of God: and they that resist shall receive to themselves damnation.

Romans 13:2

You will be protected by it, covered by it, directed by it, assisted by it, and if obedient you will be honored and promoted by it. So when it comes to authority and what our relationship with it is like, it's really up to us.

For rulers are not a terror to good works, but to the evil. Wilt thou then not be afraid of the power? do that which is good, and thou shalt have praise of the same.

Romans 13:3

When it comes to rulers remember this; rulers are always necessary to bring measure and when we stay within our measure we tend to reach our destiny. True rulers don't desire to discipline, but instead to deliver us into our purpose. Our obedience or disobedience is what makes the difference. Sometimes, a lot times actually, God uses them for our correction, direction, discipline and maturation. The role of authority is to aid us in becoming sensitive in the right way to live, move and love.

Wherefore ye must needs be subject, not only for wrath, but also for conscience sake.

Romans 13:5

Therefore realizing what authority is ordained to do for us God says we ought to give those in authority all the respect that is due. Truth is, if our lives are governed by love, then there will be limits we just won't break and lines we just won't cross.

Love worketh no ill to his neighbour: therefore love is the fulfilling of the law.

And that, knowing the time, that now it is high time to awake out of sleep: for now is our salvation nearer than when we believed.

Romans 13:10-11

For those of us who are in authority in our homes, remember God's proof of real leadership is our level of service.

But Jesus called them unto him, and said, Ye know that the princes of the Gentiles exercise dominion over them, and they that are great exercise authority upon them.

But it shall not be so among you: but whosoever will be great among you, let him be your minister;

And whosoever will be chief among you, let him be your servant.

Matthew 20:25-27

Just listen to the leadership statement of Jesus found in Matthew 20:28. He didn't come to receive, He came to give something, and He did by and through the spirit of servant leadership. So the greatest in the house is the greatest servant in the house. How do you serve? How do you help at your house?

One that ruleth well his own house, having his children in subjection with all gravity.

I Timothy 3:4

Guys listen, the reality is that the All-Powerful, All-Wonderful, All-Everything showed up on earth serving as a baby in a family. What is it that you can't be for God to use you to get people delivered spiritually, advance His kingdom ministry and live in a way that the He alone could and would to get glory. This is called ministry. Ministry at it's greatest equals service, don't believe me, just check out King Jesus.

Now before the feast of the passover, when Jesus knew that his hour was come that he should depart out of this world unto the Father, having loved his own which were in the world, he loved them unto the end.

John 13:1

Serving exemplifies love, and that love is given without time limitations. Love and service are at their best when there is no insecurity in us.

Jesus knowing that the Father had given all things into his hands, and that he was come from God, and went to God.

John 13:3

When we are confident about our own relationship with the Lord Jesus and all he has given us, that is when we are at our best. Service is the easiest thing to get from us. It's what makes humility apparent, when we can lay aside our titles or positions for the sake of the needs of God's kingdom. When we take up the towel and put aside the robe to lay aside the things that cover us and use them for God's people and God's purpose. When we can take what we have and use it to help or cause wholeness to be released in someone's life through us. Jesus informs Peter that if you can't handle the humility I require of you, then you won't have relationship with me or be used in great authority. This swiftly sways Peter to become a very humble brother. Our authority is best seen through our humility.

Simon Peter saith unto him, Lord, not my feet only, but also my hands and my head.

John 13:9

"Home Work for Him"

Leading Through Accountability

- Set up a weekly or bi-weekly meeting with your wife. Not to last longer than thirty-five or forty minutes. Have designated topics of conversation prepared such as finances, parenting, children's needs, household needs, upcoming events, trips etc.
- Set up time for monthly or bi-monthly family meetings. Inform children of your decisions from parental meetings. This is also a means of keeping in touch with everyone.
- Establish set limits of spending when separate, establish a call amount (amount we need to call about before spending) Establish saving amount weekly, also an emergency fund amount.
- Let her know when you can, what you are doing, where you're at and if you're running late, call home (help a sister's heart).
- Place yourself under some relationships of accountability for you and your family, whether they be at church, work, or friendships with people that have convictions and Godly intentions.

Leading in Intimacy

- The meetings will help here, they will help bring you both onto the same page. Then develop a habit of asking her questions about what is happening in her world. Her friends, family, parents, plans, etc.
- Create Date nights. Once a week or bi-weekly for just you and her, no children! Remember what that was like? Yes, go

to a movie, shopping, play, or just out to eat and talk with no distractions.

- Do lunches. When you can arrange the same time, steal away in midday or plan an afternoon off. Sometimes my wife and I would just get in the car and ride to Baltimore Harbor and get back just as our kids would be getting off the bus.
- Bring her flowers, her favorite candy, cards for no reason or something that reminds you both of your last trip together.
- Take a vacation away together, go somewhere THAT IS NOT HERE!!! Have some fun! Go do nothing together.

Leading in Humility

- Be the first to say I'm sorry, and the first to repent *and mean it*. Allow her to share without interrupting, take the truth like a man, and change where needed.
- When wrong, confess it, not just sorry, but sorry for what exactly?
- Challenge yourself to be one of, if not the biggest servant in the house (and yes, that means do some house work or cook or something, you live there too).
- Find ways to serve your wife and your family, "whosoever is chief is servant".
- At the next time of intense fellowship (argument), try to listen and not interrupt (you take the high road).

Leading in Initiative and Responsibility

- Plan time for you and your wife, then time for you and you family, have certain days you are HOME!

- Try to put a time line on your wife's desires around the house, try not to let things linger. Call somebody!
- Make an action plan and stick to it.
- Initiate prayer time with your family, not deep just let everyone pray, then you pray.
- Lead in addressing problems and giving solutions for the household, if her's are better it just means you were smart to marry her!

Leading in Authority

- Authority starts when we begin to cover, protect and take responsibility for our wives and family.
- It means we are the first response and first defense when situations get tense.
- Authority never steps on, over or past the other person. It's goal is to get everyone in step for the same purpose.
- God's Word says we both have to submit in and for the relationship.

Submitting yourselves one to another in the fear of God.

Ephesians 5:21

- Authority has to be willing to make the tough and hard decisions, even when everyone won't like them. (seek true peace, not false peace).
- True authority doesn't seek to discipline but deliver those under its covering. You are the umbrella.

CHAPTER ONE: **THE MINISTRY OF THE LEADER**

"The best investment in your future is proper influence today"

~ John Maxwell

CHAPTER TWO

THE MINISTRY OF THE INFLUENCER (WIFE)

Please do not discount the word influence or the term influencer. It is the power of lovingly aiding, shaping, impacting, imparting, and affecting by expressing opinions, guidance and suggestions. This is done with the intent of supporting and guiding someone towards a favorable decision or direction, and still much more than that. Many times you as women can cause a major shift within visions, missions, purpose and/or relationships. Let me be clear, I am not talking about manipulation or the art of using ones flesh to affect another's thoughts, steps or purpose for the benefit of oneself. Influence is using one's wisdom, instruction, and communication in fulfilling the same mission or vision with another. To influence is to earn the respect of another and the right to advise through living, loving, and listening as well as relating with this other person.

Having influence with someone is not an overnight process. You will be trusted in areas where another can't see, doesn't know, is hindered, struggles with how to lead, and at times may be left ignorant or in need of assurance. When you tap into this, you discover one of the greatest strengths of a woman in affecting situations for change. We can look to an Esther whose influence was positioned to save a nation. Through influence Abigail saves her life and that of her husband. By influence Zipporah saved Moses from God's judgment and destruction. With her influence Deborah, a woman of influence, gives needed assurance to Barak, a man of influence himself.

This same influence can be a negative, a woman could affect in the manner in which Delilah influenced Samson, possibly to the point he loses vision, makes poor decisions, even forsakes his mission. You have a woman like Jezebel, who influenced Ahab to the point that she controlled him and the entire kingdom. A wife also has power as the influencer of the family's future. Will you be like Eve and influence your family out of the will of God, or like Hannah, the mother of the great judge Samuel, and influence them into the will of God? You see, a Godly influencer will always cause others to be pushed toward God's will for their world or toward a better standard in their lives. A positive influencer will grant assurance to those submitted to her, make a difference in the lives of those around her and increase the substance of those she's submitted to. She releases deliverance through her heart.

The disparity between the influencer and the manipulator is this; the manipulator is only involved in the situation for some form of personal satisfaction or gain. Manipulation is all about getting your will done regardless of the will, word or ways of God. The major question is this, do you want your will or God's to be done?

INFLUENCING THROUGH SUPPORT

The influence begins with your support. Support is a small word but holds great power, for without support the Golden Gate bridge would collapse, without support the Empire State Building would crumple, without support homes would become a heap of wood and aluminum. Support is one of the strongest supplements of life and strength. Where would the Leaning Tower of Pisa be without those supports that lean? Even though they're leaning, they still keep that historical landmark upright. You see, no matter how awesome a vision or mission may be, without the necessary support system it ends up only a dream. Someone has to be strong enough, wise enough, and balanced enough to conceive it and carry it to the point of birthing it. Then choose to aid it, nurture it and help grow it into its fullness. You do that with your support. Know this, just as Eve was fitted and tailored for Adam you are fitted and tailored for your Adam. While you may appear soft like a pillow, your strength is like a marble pillar standing, uncompromising, unyielding, unwavering, always remaining in a position of support and influence. In Genesis 2:18 although the vision is given to Adam, he dreams it, visualizes it, and sees it, it is Eve who becomes the conceiver, carrier, and helps to give birth to it. She is the one gifted to nurture it, incubate and care for it. She has been created as the helpmeet for the vision.

The term helpmeet is used to describe you and your purpose. It means one suited, tailor made, so realize she is not off the rack, but she is tailor made and custom ordered. Like a tailor made suit (of a high value & quality) you convey definition, character, distinction, enhancement and influence as well as substance to and for kingdom business. Many times we see houses, and they may be beautiful on the outside, but in reality the hidden strength lies on the inside with the beams that cause the house to stand.

I would like to state here that there is a distinction made for the one who is assigned to have that level of access to our destiny. The definition is not just any woman but the one woman called wife. Being tailor made also means being gifted and created to cover one another; to enhance, cause a difference or create influence. What Armani would do for a man is what an anointed help meet will do for him: aid in defining and adding to his being. Just any old suit off the rack won't do, no matter how good the sale price is! This is what my very own wife has brought to my life. While I have the vision, Bernadette is the key person that aids and adds to my vision, as well as assists bringing it to completion or fruition. That's both in family and in the ministry. I never have to guess if she has my heart or my back for that matter. She's built for covering the weaknesses, the areas where I lose focus, and the injuries I've never shared with anyone else. It is a calling, the helpmeet brings a different level of discerning, feeling, seeing, and responding to the table. Usually it's for our own protection, even though we think we're the tough ones.

Another thing… according to the promises of God, when a man finds a wife (note to my singles; she's not hunting, but being hunted) he finds a good thing and obtains favor with God. The challenge becomes learning to receive her with all this gifting and not see it as competition but completion. Don't see her as one against, but as one sent to bring to pass the God given assignment for both of you. Unfortunately as men we sometimes suffer from "the mind and mode of competition". Men have this erroneous mentality that anyone who comes too close to us is against us rather than for us. We don't realize that it's a childish mindset, and it's one of the things that delay our purpose and God's best for our lives.

Abraham was promised a son from God at an old age. Now Abraham can want the promise, but without Sarah he will never produce a son by himself. Like Moses, he could lead it, but alone he would have ended up doubting it, or being frustrated by the very thing he's called to lead. We hinder the vision many times because we simply don't let her in on it, don't pull her into agreement with it. What would be a practical definition of the wife we're talking about; someone who has committed her life to you, is willing to try and understand you when you don't understand you, still chooses to honor you, hold you, forgive you, and see the best in you after she's seen the worst in you, and still love you inspite of you. It means being willing do all this lovingly yet with real accountability, not letting you get off easy. She is also someone with her own identity, personality, security, and individuality. She has her own creativity and ability to communicate her ideas, dreams and desires clearly. A wife is a woman who is for your life.

House and riches are the inheritance of fathers: and a prudent wife is from the LORD.

Proverbs 19:14

Who can find a virtuous woman? for her price is far above rubies. The heart of her husband doth safely trust in her, so that he shall have no need of spoil. She will do him good and not evil all the days of her life. She seeketh wool, and flax, and worketh willingly with her hands. She is like the merchants' ships; she bringeth her food from afar. She riseth also while it is yet night, and giveth meat to her household, and a portion to her maidens. She considereth a field, and buyeth it: with the fruit of her hands she planteth a vineyard. She girdeth her loins with strength, and strengtheneth her arms. She perceiveth that her merchandise is good: her candle goeth not out by night.

She layeth her hands to the spindle, and her hands hold the distaff. She stretcheth out her hand to the poor; yea, she reacheth forth her hands to the needy. She is not afraid of the snow for her household: for all her household are clothed with scarlet. She maketh herself coverings of tapestry; her clothing is silk and purple. Her husband is known in the gates, when he sitteth among the elders of the land. She maketh fine linen, and selleth it; and delivereth girdles unto the merchant. Strength and honour are her clothing; and she shall rejoice in time to come.

She openeth her mouth with wisdom; and in her tongue is the law of kindness. She looketh well to the ways of her household, and eateth not the bread of idleness. Her children arise up, and call her blessed; her husband also, and he praiseth her. Many daughters have done virtuously, but thou excellest them all. Favour is deceitful, and beauty is vain: but a woman that feareth the LORD, she shall be praised. Give her of the fruit of her hands; and let her own works praise her in the gates.

Proverbs 31:10-31

The same thing she does with children is the same thing she can do with the vision; carry it, nurture it, birth it and help raise it. You see there are different types of women. Let's break them down:

1. *The "Hoochie"*

She only uses the influence of her body to get what she wants, lacks or needs personally no matter what.(Herodias)

2. *The "Holla Back Girl"*

She wants to appear like the hoochie, but she's not really like that, her focus is on what you do for her, or what she can get from you. If she can't get it, she'll leave quick (she'll holla back).

3. *"Miss Hindrance"*

This is a woman without her own vision and direction, but through affection and attention she delays, robs or kills another's vision.(see Delilah)

4. *"Half-Timer"*

Half the time she's in the church and half the time she's in the world. She's up and down, in and out, she may have issues of being schizophrenic. This causes her to compromise and waiver and keeps her from the blessing or God given benefits.

5. *"Holy Woman"*

Fine, not just in her appearance, but in her essence and her very substance. She carries a major level of influence. She comes committed, submitted, respected and attractive in looks and in life. She is led by

God because she lives for God. Just as the woman in Proverbs 31, her difference is in the power of her influence, service and strength.

The question is, which one is the closest resemblance to who you see in the mirror?

INFLUENCING THROUGH HONOR

To honor is to lift one up above others, including you; to esteem one in the midst of others, to give priority and response to immediately. Honor is derived from the word honorarium, meaning having worth, value or weight. If in any way you find yourself continually comparing your husband to your father, grandfather or uncles as a way of measuring, you may be in danger of dishonoring him. You may also miss the God-given originality and uniqueness that has been placed within him as God's man for you. It means a world of difference for you to hear him, meaning you receive his words and listen to his heart. It also means not holding his way of doing things against previous headship that you have experienced. Seeing him spiritually and respecting him physically, acknowledging his position and admiring him as a Son in the Kingdom of God.

That's the difference between living around him and living with him. If you are just living around him, you will make major decisions without him and change decisions without his consideration or notification. You make little of the ideas, thoughts, suggestions or opinions that come from him. You can tell when a man's honor has been wounded when his response is muted, disregarded or aborted. Honoring him is weighing and giving weight to his comments, thoughts and input against your own and others, and doing so with a willingness to submit if God, your spirit or heart agrees with him.

Now, to weigh something is to allow it to have an affect on our will, mind and our natural inclination. A wife who honors her husband has the ability to honor both the man and the position he holds so that God will honor her. We can look back at how Abigail honored David and God honored her. When truly honoring someone you give your abilities, creativity, ingenuity, and yourself physically and mentally in many ways. Honor is not just given based on what is done, but also it is to be given because it is due.

Render therefore to all their dues: tribute to whom tribute is due; custom to whom custom; fear to whom fear; honour to whom honour.

Romans 13:7

You do it already, every day at your job. You may not like your boss but you give them honor, you respect and obey them. In all honesty you may not feel the repect , but you will it. If we can do it for those we don't love, how much the more should we make that sacrifice for those we love and we know love us.

Nevertheless let every one of you in particular so love his wife even as himself; and the wife see that she reverence her husband.

Ephesians 5:33

Note: This is not by an external force but by your internal faith. To respect and give reverence is something that the wife must make a conscious effort to do. This is accomplished by noticing him, regarding him, loving him, and by praising him publicly and privately.

Render therefore to all their dues: tribute to whom tribute is due; custom to whom custom; fear to whom fear; honour to whom honour.

Romans 13:7

To render means to give what is due. One of the best gifts one can give is to give someone the honor due them. What is due speaks to what is expected, as in the rent is due on the 1st. You see, it's not about how I *feel* or think, it is expected. How many of us *feel* like paying the rent or mortgage? Go ahead do what you *feel* like doing. It won't be too long before you begin *feeling* differently. So to honor him is to value his wants, words, and needs that are in line with the will of God. This is what you both agreed to, for better or for worse. Find ways to thank and appreciate him. Create expressions of worth for him, and he will for you.

In contrast, to dishonor is to strip of the honor given, to disrespect or to discredit. This can be done with damaging comments or sarcasm; "That was so stupid", "That was dumb", "anybody can do that". When a woman says things of that nature, a man hears that he's stupid, he's dumb, and that he's not a Man in your eyes with regard to whatever the issue is you were speaking of. It is your respect for his words, wants, work and will that tells him whether or not you love and honor him. In a survey from the book "Love & Respect" by Dr. Emerson Eggeriches men stated that they would rather live with a woman that honored and respected them, than a woman that loved them but did not respect them. Remember, your boss is not your husband, but you respect him. Your pastor is not your husband, but you respect him. And yes, your father is not your husband, yet you learned and chose to respect him. So, when it comes to the man you love, how do you respect him? Do you value his decisions, emotions, opinions and his dreams? One way to do a self-check is to sincerely ask yourself, "Would I have been willing to receive and respond to what my husband said if someone else had said it?"

Also, remember not to devalue him in front of your friends, his friends, or family. Don't speak for him, but let him share his opinion. Don't change family decisions without his insight, consideration and input.

INFLUENCING BY WAY OF YOUR LIFE

One of the greatest ways to show honor is by being willing to produce change in your life. By sometimes giving up your ways and your will a husband knows that his words, wants, will and works carry weight with you. Unity is demonstrated when your will matches up with his. This brings on a situation that releases what we call mutual respect. You can also change your words, ways, or walk. Then that influence can be seen by way of the tangible evidence that is your life. Remember, change never begins with those around you. Rather, it begins within you. In your life his heart means more than what the world can do for or offer you. Your influence is felt through decisions, mannerisms and subjection. Know this while we're here, subjection is reserved only for those called husband; not my friend, baby or boo or any other level of acquaintance outside that of God's marriage covenant.

When we look at subjection, we see sub; meaning not just under control, but under emotional and relational control of yourself. Then we have -ject, to have input, share in the action, participation in situations. Even though you are under subjection, you still have access to all decisions for the family with a level of authority. You may not have the final authority, but the desired result is unity. You may also know this, if what you share (ject) is not received or acted on, it does not mean you were rejected. It only means that your suggestion this time was not the final decision.

Influence by way of life means living in such a Christ-centered way, that your life becomes infectious, affecting and literally intoxicating those who are watching. The life of Christ in you becomes contagious to the point that your husband, children, and anyone in connection with you want this Jesus. It expressly becomes so overwhelming to them that it initiates transformation in everyone within your sphere of influence. Wow, it's a life that can win others to Jesus without mumbling a word. Through loving, serving, forgiving, releasing and honoring them you draw them to Him. It's a life like Ruth's, they heard of her commitment, honor, service and love for Naomi and it forced everyone around to take notice. Even to the extent that Boaz heard of her before he ever saw her, and had already determined her worthy of attention, provision, connection, protection and the covenant of marriage. He wanted her honor to be his honor, her commitment to be his commitment, her level of service to be his service, and her love to be his love.

Likewise, ye wives, be in subjection to your own husbands; that, if any obey not the word, they also may without the word be won by the conversation of the wives.

I Peter 3:1

We must also note that it is not just the physical splendor that attracts, but the spirit also pulls the spirit.

Deep calleth unto deep at the noise of thy waterfalls: All thy waves and thy billows are gone over me.

Psalm 42:7

When we look at the life of another, it is the inward person not the outward that allows us to see God's Son.

But let it be the hidden man of the heart, in that which is not corruptible, even the ornament of a meek and quiet spirit, which is in the sight of God of great price.

I Peter 3:4

Maybe it's through the influence of a life that you and I will draw family members to Christ.

For what knowest thou, O wife, whether thou shalt save thy husband? or how knowest thou, O man, whether thou shalt save thy wife?

I Corinthians 7:16

Nabal to Abgail, Artaxerxes to Ester to Boaz, Mary to Joseph.

INFLUENCING THROUGH SUBMISSION
(Oh No, Not the "S" Word!)

So many times the word submission is erroneously defined, demanded, improperly displayed as well as mistakenly defended. The word submission is the word hopotasso, which means lining up under, lining up with and/or lining up for. Submission has nothing to do with being stepped on, stepped over or stepped past, specifically if it is based on ones natural gender, physical color or any other overrated trait. Submission is important for many reasons. One of which is that it reveals our respect or lack thereof for spiritual order and authority, and in doing so reveals ones own spiritual authority, power and maturity. Oh, and by the way, that power is only biblically authorized to make oneself submit.

Humble yourselves in the sight of the Lord, and he shall lift you up.
James 4:10

We are not talking about losing your identity, giving up your individuality, nor falsely subjecting yourself to some form of modern day slavery. Beloved, for the kingdom to be what it needs to be, for our cities to be what they are supposed to be, for our families to reveal who they are called to be as a light to the world, and for our ministries to be effective and affect change for God's glory, we need you woman of God. We need you wife, sister, mother, daughter and friend to be who God has called you to be: none other than the creative, left brain thinking, emotion having, famine celebrating, family raising, career evolving, class teaching, ministry leading, powerfully preaching, detail oriented, gifted, anointed and unique you that God made you.

We are talking about operating, may I say, willfully operating in humility and unity that will bring about God's immutable glory. Submission is yielding and aligning for the fulfilling of what God is asking and wanting. We must be properly aligned, like a company in the Army has a ranking, Private, Sergeant and Lieutenant, etc. all with their own gifting, calling, and specialized anointing. At the commander's order, "Attention!", they bring themselves into alignment for the fulfillment of a greater assignment. A mission that is much bigger than anything that they personally may have going on. They choose to submit themselves for the sake of unity to gain the victory.

Submitting yourselves one to another in the fear of God.

Ephesians 5:21

So it is that we, and I said we, men and women must take on the responsibility to bring ourselves in to spiritual alignment. On to you our sister, the battle of submission is almost always partly due to the makeup of the other person in authority. However, based on biblical scriptural authority, you are the only person that hinders your own submission.

Yes, I know he has blown it, missed the mark and at times couldn't hit water if he fell out of a boat. Tracking his hits and misses is not your responsibility in the matter, nor is it your job to constantly and regularly remind him of his shortcomings. The last time I checked, the Holy Spirit was the only one given permission to bring about conviction that will cause transformation. That stuff you're doing, it may just be called nagging (I'm just saying…).

The goal of the submission is to bring about a yielding that causes two wills to mesh into one will, two minds to become one mind, two hearts to become one heart and two persons to have one vision. We're talking unity here. So submission for both of us has more to do with getting oneself into position to bring forth God's vision and fulfill His promise. It's when we line up that God tends to show up, our world goes up, and our agreement breaks up the plots, plans and schemes of the enemy. Again, this is not about getting stepped over, stepped on or stepped past, but getting in step with God, your husband, the vision of God in your church, and the vocation for your life. No one can make you submit but you, just as no one can make you yield but you.

Humble yourselves in the sight of the Lord, and he shall exalt you.

James 4:10

If we ever figured out that the way for all of us to get victory is like Jesus, we must submit our talents, strengths, gifts, anointing and calling to a greater authority, wow would we be dangerous. Here are some hard truths about submission, whatever area we can't walk in submission in, we will never receive celebration in that area. As soon as Jesus submitted and came down from heaven, there was celebration in earth and heaven. The celebration didn't have to wait for Him to do a miracle or to be risen from the dead on the third day. The victory was received as soon as His life was submitted to a God whose plans can never fail. Where there is no submission, there is no way of getting true validation or recognition.

And Jesus, when he was baptized, went up straightway out of the water: and, lo, the heavens were opened unto him, and he saw the Spirit of God descending like a dove, and lighting upon him:
And lo a voice from heaven, saying, This is my beloved Son, in whom I am well pleased.

Matthew 3:16-17

Here we see Jesus at His baptism. His submission was the key to His confirmation, next level of position, and release to His mission.

Then was Jesus led up of the Spirit into the wilderness to be tempted of the devil.

Matthew 4:1

Jesus submits to be led to the desert and returns with authority and power afterward. No submission hinders you from new levels of elevation and promotion.

That at the name of Jesus every knee should bow, of things in heaven and things on earth and things under the earth.

Philippians 2:10

*Wives, **be in subjection** unto your own husbands, as unto the Lord.*

Ephesians 5:22

Know this, Jesus' secret weapon was his submission.

*But as the church is subject to Christ, so **let** the wives also **be** to their husbands in everything.*

Ephesians 5:24

Practically speaking, what does the church do? They recognize Him, receive Him, commit to relating to Him and confess their faults and sin to Him. The church must raise Him to a level where He has no peers. They render service to Him, heap upon Him gifts and release praise to Him, and they alone rest in the love that only He can give. We do this with Jesus but do we try this with the one in covenant with us.

And being found in fashion as a man, he humbled himself, and became obedient unto death, even the death of the cross.

Wherefore God also hath highly exalted him, and given him a name which is above every name.

Philippians 2:8-9

This scripture reveals something about the levels of our obedience. Based on this passage Christ's elevation, ascension, magnification, and glorification were directly proportionate to his level of submission. Remember that Jesus' submission proceeded being raised in the power of resurrection.

"Home Work for Her"

Influence Through Support

- How do you add to him?
- How do you aid in assisting him with the vision?
- How do you support him?
- How do you cover what others don't see?
- Do you find yourself competing with him?
- Does he know that you are there for him? If so, how?
- Have you let him know you desire to help him?
- What are the areas that you can't support due to not being in agreement?
- Have you addressed these areas?
- Do you see similarities between your own behavior and that of the types of women we dealt with? Of the types of women we dealt with, which one are you?
- How do you help?
- How do you hold up? Hold on?
- Has he given you your part to play?

Influence Through Honor

- Name three ways you lift him up.
- When was the last time you publicly honored him in front of family or friends?
- How do you honor his words or his heart's desire?
- Do you include him in your major decisions?
- Do you ask his opinion? (or do you talk to him after your decisions)
- Do you change decisions you made with him, without notifying him?
- Do you weigh his opinions, instruction, comments or thoughts?
- Do you withhold your abilities, creativity or thoughts?
- In what ways do you honor his, words, will,(thoughts and emotions) and wants?
- Have you let him know you appreciate and value him? (not just on Father's Day, or a birthday)

Influence by Way of Your Life

- How have you given your worth, weight or your will to aid him in the way he should go?
- In what way has your life been a good influence on him?
- How is your life infecting and affecting those around you?
- How has your life caused him to be drawn to Jesus?

"Even the happiest child has moments when he wishes his parents were dead"

~ Allen Fromme

CHAPTER THREE

PARENTING 101

Being a parent is, at times, overwhelming, trying, stretching and all-together tiring. Honestly, there are times when it is flat-out frustrating. Yet at the same time parenting is exciting, exhilarating, rewarding, satisfying and incredibly humbling. This is when we come to understand our role and responsibility for and to our children and the families that they will produce. Both now and in the future it is and will be as I said, humbling. As a parent, I see it as my God given mission to love, receive, raise, relate, train, teach, discipline and disciple them. I must impart wisdom, aid in decisions, give direction, prepare for separation, as well as be a living demonstration. It's these things that humble me parentally. God has literally entrusted them to me on a temporary basis. None of the following are negative in and of themselves, but day care, afterschool programs, regular school, clubs, sports, boy scouts and girl scouts, grandma or grandpa will never be given the primary responsibility for any one of my children.

Understand me, parenting is God's chosen, given, elected and selected method of early growth and development and you and I are His chosen vessels. In other words, being a parent is a God given assignment.

Lo, children are an heritage of the LORD: and the fruit of the womb is his reward.

As arrows are in the hand of a mighty man; so are children of the youth.

Happy is the man that hath his quiver full of them: they shall not be ashamed, but they shall speak with the enemies in the gate.

Psalm 127:3-5

Note this, we all have the necessary equipment, but we must choose to, agree, to reject or accept the assignment. There is a weight that we bear if we don't parent.

And I will give children to be their princes, and babes shall rule over them.

And the people shall be oppressed, every one by another, and every one by his neighbour: the child shall behave himself proudly against the ancient, and the base against the honourable.

As for my people, children are their oppressors, and women rule over them. O my people, they which lead thee cause thee to err, and destroy the way of thy paths.

Isaiah 3:4-5,12

These verses represent a lot of what see in our community at the present time. Events such as the Columbine and Virginia Tech shootings, even what recently happened in, of all places, Lancaster, PA speak to the reality and necessity of intentionally accepting and embracing our roles as parents. We have to evaluate our own parental state. Let's take a look at a few different types of parents:

Passive – This parent is generally indifferent; always agreeing with or yielding to the child for sake of not fighting. They may see but will not confront, address or challenge. The root of the problem is the parent's own fear of rejection. Samuel was this type of parent. He was quicker to correct Saul or the people of their error than he was to correct his own children.

Aggressive – This is the pharaoh type leader. They are hard, rigid, accepting nothing but excellence. They are always disciplining, pushing, correcting, always judging, ever controlling and rarely hearing. This is usually the result of having been controlled themselves, raised in a micro-managed childhood, or possibly a simple result of their own pride.

Inactive – This parent is present but inattentive, indifferent, irrelevant and ignorant to the child's issues. To them the child is an inconvenience. Fear of their own failures sometimes cause an unwillingness to face up to our children and the responsibility that comes along with parenthood –David was such.

Manipulative – The manipulative parent governs for their own satisfaction, pleasure, or gratification. They are only active for their own motives –"I'll do this for you IF you do this for me…"Their own feelings and interests control how they treat their children. Jacob treated Joseph differently than his brothers for his own reasons – his love of Rachel above his other wife and concubines, and his pride at fathering a child in his old age.

Parenting habits and traits (both good and bad) tend to be repetitive. If we do not consciously acknowledge them and decide to accept the good and deny the bad, we will most often repeat the same mistakes. When we acknowledge even the bad in the proper light, we can learn from it, and work to change it.

Effective – Effective parenting is leadership with the intent to love and propel your child into a happy and successful future. It is being committed to be present, find the child's strengths, goals and direction and make the required investments for them to reach their destination. It means being willing to change; learn about being a parent. It means always learning, listening, addressing, loving, adapting, training and when needed repenting. It means doing this through the ages and stages of a child's life: infancy, toddler, adolescent, pre-teen, teen, young adult, adult; willingly moving them from dependence to interdependence to independence. Let's visit those ages and stages, before we launch into our mission. Let's check the foundation.

PARENTING WITH GOD'S MENTALITY

I was once told that parenting didn't come with a book of instructions. The truth is that the book had already been written. It's just that we may not have given it the right attention. Our mentality is shaped by our history, family, personal beliefs and what we view in society. The only challenge with these is that all of them are subject to the fact that God in his divinity is He that created humanity. Humanity did not create itself. Parenting is again more of an assignment. It's not for enjoyment, entertainment, punishment, confinement or building our own self-monument. It's given positionally. It's going to take longevity. It means deciding to persevere and be effective. To do that, one must be an active parent.

The word "parent" comes from *the Greek word* "**pa**" (or "**para**" meaning – "one alongside to aid, assist, aim; "paraklete" which means you have been sent alongside to guide directly into destiny; gift to give what is needed and of necessity; aid to heal– like paramedic knowledge; advocate for– like a paralegal; help in falls– like a parachute) and the Greek word "**rent**" (meaning temporary-position for destiny). The word literally describes someone who is gifted and ordained for the purpose of preparing a young person from infancy to maturity for destiny.

Lo, children are an heritage of the LORD: and the fruit of the womb is his reward.

Psalm 127:3

Every time we see a child, God shows us a part of himself, and His parental nature.

And God said, Let us make man in our image, after our likeness: and let them have dominion over the fish of the sea, and over the fowl of the air, and over the cattle, and over all the earth, and over every creeping thing that creepeth upon the earth.

Genesis 1:26

God has given us the authority, ability, mentality, and energy to raise our children, prepare them for destiny and bring God glory. God promises never to give you and I what we can't handle, so we are more than able to do this. God will never give you an assignment without giving you the equipment or the enablement for it. As a parent we must see our children in the same Godly covenant.

And I will establish my covenant between me and thee and thy seed after thee in their generations for an everlasting covenant, to be a God unto thee, and to thy seed after thee.

Genesis 17:7

We must not only see them as our children, but see them for the signs and wonders that God calls them.

Behold, I and the children whom the LORD hath given me are for signs and for wonders in Israel from the LORD of hosts, which dwelleth in mount Zion.

Isaiah 8:18

God sees the assignment. He knows our involvement, but He also sees the fulfillment of the assignment. We see our baby. God sees that child mature, defeating the enemy and taking kingdom territory.

As arrows are in the hand of a mighty man; so are children of the youth.

Psalm 127:4

We see struggles and obstacles for our children to overcome – many we try to keep them from. He sees the obstacles that they struggled with and overcame with His help; the battles and victories that gained territory and equipped them to be a blessing to others.

See, I have this day set thee over the nations and over the kingdoms, to root out, and to pull down, and to destroy, and to throw down, to build, and to plant.

Jeremiah 1:10

PARENTING OUR CHILDREN IN INFANCY

The scriptures tell us that God knew us before we knew ourselves.

Before I formed thee in the belly I knew thee; and before thou camest forth out of the womb I sanctified thee, and I ordained thee a prophet unto the nations.

Jeremiah 1:5

Before anyone else ever thought of us, before we had a body or friends or family, before our parents looked longingly in each other's eyes God knew us. Before there was ever iniquity or sin to our charge, He knew us and gave us life. Even more importantly, before we committed our first sin God knew what we would do. And before one act, fault, fall or failure from us, He died for us. This is the God who loved us and he gave us a family. It's incredible to realize that we were on his mind all the time.

What is man, that thou art mindful of him? and the son of man, that thou visitest him?

Psalm 8:4

God thought so much of us that He designed a specific family just for each of us. He created a family for us, and a divine plan.

See, I have this day set thee over the nations and over the kingdoms, to root out, and to pull down, and to destroy, and to throw down, to build, and to plant.

Jeremiah 1:10

On top of all that was mentioned, God also plans strength for us for this time of parenting. Yes, even through the crying, whining, diaper changing, and sleep loss, He sustains us. It is with this strength God gives us for loving, shaping, forming, consecrating, that we can be effective parents. This season is need driven; they have needs – we become driven. Our children, just as other biblical children, have been given a destiny and it begins even while in infancy. Understand that in this season we have the greatest influence in and over them. This not just in teaching them motor skills and physical movements, but also in exposing them to spiritual songs, positive words and healthy environments. Whether it's songs of worship or reading the word of God to them, we begin shaping and molding them. It is our role to guide and cover them just as God says He does for them.

For thou hast possessed my reins: thou hast covered me in my mother's womb.

I will praise thee; for I am fearfully and wonderfully made: marvellous are thy works; and that my soul knoweth right well.

My substance was not hid from thee, when I was made in secret, and curiously wrought in the lowest parts of the earth.

Thine eyes did see my substance, yet being unperfect; and in thy book all my members were written, which in continuance were fashioned, when as yet there was none of them.

How precious also are thy thoughts unto me, O God! how great is the sum of them!

Psalm 139:13-17

One of the best things we can do is pray for them daily and eventually dedicate them back to the King of the Kingdom. If it was good for Jesus, than it should still be good for us.

And when the days of her purification according to the law of Moses were accomplished, they brought him to Jerusalem, to present him to the Lord; (As it is written in the law of the LORD, Every male that openeth the womb shall be called holy to the Lord;) And to offer a sacrifice according to that which is said in the law of the Lord, A pair of turtledoves, or two young pigeons. And, behold, there was a man in Jerusalem, whose name was Simeon; and the same man was just and devout, waiting for the consolation of Israel: and the Holy Ghost was upon him.

And it was revealed unto him by the Holy Ghost, that he should not see death, before he had seen the Lord's Christ. And he came by the Spirit into the temple: and when the parents brought in the child Jesus, to do for him after the custom of the law, Then took he him up in his arms, and blessed God, and said, Lord, now lettest thou thy servant depart in peace, according to thy word: For mine eyes have seen thy salvation,

Which thou hast prepared before the face of all people; A light to lighten the Gentiles, and the glory of thy people Israel. And Joseph and his mother marvelled at those things which were spoken of him. And Simeon blessed them, and said unto Mary his mother, Behold, this child is set for the fall and rising again of many in Israel; and for a sign which shall be spoken against; (Yea, a sword shall pierce through thy own soul also,) that the thoughts of many hearts may be revealed.

And there was one Anna, a prophetess, the daughter of Phanuel, of the tribe of Aser: she was of a great age, and had lived with an husband seven years from her virginity; And she was a widow of about fourscore and four years, which departed not from the temple, but served God with fastings and prayers night and day. And she coming in that instant gave thanks likewise unto the Lord, and spake of him to all them that looked for redemption in Jerusalem.

Luke 2:22-38

Dedicating a child to God was a sign of devotion and appreciation to God for His decision to grant them this child. For all of our children we have the natural goals of seeing them crawl, hear, look up, sit up and grow up. But we as an effective parent desires to see the Lord show up in them.

PARENTING OUR CHILDREN AS TODDLERS – 2-5

I'm not sure if they are called toddlers at this stage due to their toddling style of walking, or the fact that now some of the innocence is shifting, the child's will begins to show and their perfect state is starting to toddle over. They begin revealing they have a will, by the way it's not normally the same as mine or yours. They begin speaking. That's good. But when they start repeating the things we'd rather they didn't it now requires some training and coaching. Please do not allow their cuteness to become a ploy for a limitless and thoughtless communication process. What one might find funny at three is sometimes abusive and can cause injury at thirteen. It's during this toddler season they discover new words, like "no", "don't want to", "mine". It's during this time they must be guided, checked and redirected to understand who has the proper authority in the family. The longer you wait the stronger their will (and their capacity to defy you), will grow. Their teaching is by us both intentionally and unintentionally. I believe we are and should be our children's first teachers.

Personally, our children all knew how to read and write their alphabet and numbers before they were exposed to another teacher. They knew addition and subtraction before they ever entered a real classroom. I believe we should lay the foundation and the educational system should build on that one.

This causes three major things:

1. The birth of great intellect.

2. Increased confidence.

3. A higher degree of self-respect.

Part of the assignment of our parental diligence is to establish as strong a foundation as possible. We are called to love and build them when we feel like it, and when we don't, when we're tired and when we're not tired. It is the same with spiritual devotions and consistently asking them to pray. "What does God think about that? What would Jesus do?" It is intentionally singing godly songs around them, listening to Godly music with them in the car, at home, while cleaning, washing, cooking. This brings about a God consciousness. We should initiate it and require it. This teaches them to perceive it as the norm. Now, this also requires that they actually see you doing the same thing.

And thou shalt teach them diligently unto thy children, and shalt talk of them when thou sittest in thine house, and when thou walkest by the way, and when thou liest down, and when thou risest up.

And thou shalt bind them for a sign upon thine hand, and they shall be as frontlets between thine eyes.

And thou shalt write them upon the posts of thy house, and on thy gates.

Deuteronomy 6:7-9

It is also good to start them speaking spiritual confessions over their own lives. We do this each morning on the way to school and in our church on Sunday mornings. You may say 'are you talking about toddlers?

Yes, I am. Here is just one example of why: Through this process all five of our children chose to receive Jesus as there Savior between the ages of four and seven. And no, we didn't ask them. They asked us if they could receive Jesus.

The reality is that much in our children is the product of our parenting. It is during this season we begin molding character, attitudes, emotions, decisions, manners, respect, limitations, and teach them authority, responsibility, accountability and financially by both disciplining them and rewarding them.

Note, there is a difference between correction and punishment. Correction leads to instruction and wisdom. Punishment leads to frustration. Correction is done in love. Punishment is usually done in angered emotions. As parents we discern our children's bent and develop steps such as:

- Talking to them
- Time out
- Loss of privileges
- Loss of opportunities
- Loss of activities
- Or yes physically spanking

I trust G-O-D-not CYS (Child and Youth Services). Develop a conduct code. Place it on the refrigerator in the house. Codes like this help guide. They produce consistent expectation and fairness. They clearly lay out the consequences of specific behavior such as lying, being disrespectful, hitting, breaking curfew, skipping class, unreasonable phone usage, improper or excessive computer surfing, etc.

It is important to make any consequences both age appropriate and heart appropriate. Where there is no discipline, expect no conscience and no difference.

The word says, "Foolishness is bound up in the heart of a child and the rod of correction drives it far from him." (Proverbs 22:15) Either you are doing the driving, or they will be driving you and running your home.

Withhold not correction from the child: for if thou beatest him with the rod, he shall not die.

Thou shalt beat him with the rod, and shalt deliver his soul from hell.

Proverbs 23:13-14

The rod and reproof give wisdom: but a child left to himself bringeth his mother to shame.

Proverbs 29:15

We have to stop teaching and exposing them to adult things and issues. This also requires balance. Find ways of celebrating them: high fives, hugging, tickling, etc.

Train up a child in the way he should go: and when he is old, he will not depart from it.

Proverbs 22:6

For whom the Lord loveth he chasteneth, and scourgeth every son whom he receiveth.

Hebrews 12:6

We must see them as more than just our babies. We must ensure that they see us as more than just mommy and daddy, but as the ones God sent to lead me, guide me, check me, correct me, show life to me and give love to me.

Note: States base their growth and need of prisons by development and issues of 2nd to 4th grade children.

What are you doing to make sure they will say good things about your child?

PARENTING THROUGH ADOLESCENCE

One of the most challenging times can be (though doesn't have to be) adolescence. This particular stage is challenging because everything in our child's world is changing, and their main drive is to understand their feelings and express them. Thoughts and often comments arise like 'you don't understand me', 'this is not fair' and the 'need to express what I feel'. They now want to express their own opinion... with a lot of emotion. If they have learned negative expressions like eye rolling, neck gyrating-eye rolling, teeth-sucking-tirade having, stomping and almost dying with little to no consequence, they are going to use them.

There is a generation that curseth their father, and doth not bless their mother.

Proverbs 30:11

They're starting to struggle with their changing schools and bodies, issues of puberty and friendship as well as comparisons and new found attractions. Boys tend to change more internally and girls more externally. But all begin dealing with concerns of conformity, inferiority, and establishing their own identity. They are in the "tween" years- between being a child and being a teenager. I believe the greatest thing we can do is show them unconditional love by how we accept them, love them, support them and make ourselves available for them. We have to remember we are to train them for eventually leaving, not for remaining with us. If we allow them to live in irresponsibility they will end up with an improper level of dependence and attachment to us. Now is the time to begin giving them responsibilities, whether it's cleaning their room, a bathroom or some other weekly chore. And remember, we have to be balanced at discipline and reward so they should receive some form of allowance. With that said they also have the responsibility not do lose it by not doing the chores required of them.

This is also a great time to teach them to handle finances; such things as tithing, budgeting, giving and saving. You will have to stop following the urge to say 'I'll do it' or 'I'll take care of it'. If you do this now, prepare to continue to do the very thing you release them from for a long time. In our home one of my favorite sayings to my children is "the butler has been fired and the maid has moved on" (we never had one, but they get the message).

The reality is responsibility will produce both discipline and maturity in our children. At this age children can handle a lot of things we can, such as cleaning their rooms, making their beds, cleaning a bathroom, running a vacuum and yes even the dishes. As they receive money for this they also will reveal their heart through what they buy what they won't. They will quickly show whether they have learned to manage it or will just spend it. Now we have an opportunity to teach them how to manage it and not spend all of it.

They will also either develop our good habits in how we take care of our own home or inherit negative practices. As our kids started out they got five dollars a week for their chores. This works only for a short time, but it was a good beginning point and of course it was not enough. But as their responsibilities increased so did their income. We also created a chore day. Ours was Saturday. We cooked a delicious big breakfast first. This also drew our kids in weekly to sit down as a family. Each child eventually began taking responsibility for a part of the breakfast. After breakfast there was a ten to fifteen minute break (ok some times twenty minute break). Then it was chore time. We also created a delayed gratification factor. The work was done on Saturday, but pay day was Monday. It wasn't long, just enough not to be instant or automatic. If they desired to make more we would give them something extra to do like sweep the hall, wash the dishes or take the trash out. As they got older they graduated to things like washing the car, washing their clothes, cleaning closets etc.

Of course during this time we heavily guarded their friendships, trips and involvement with other children. That included daily asking them about what's happening in their school, class, bus trips and anything wherein they were involved. My wife actually helped me learn to listen more to what our children had to express, and it really aided my growth as a parent. It was during this season that we started sharing and dealing with peer pressures, other cultures and the realities of boy and girl desires.

If you have more than one child try as hard as you can not to compare them, or favor one of them. This saying used to help me: "what we do for one we do for all". That statement also came back to haunt me at times, particularly in ice cream lines, then toy lines then clothing lines. But I'm so glad we followed it. It held true and helped me do what I was supposed to do early. The scriptures show us very clearly the dangers of showing favoritism to your children. The story of Joseph being sold into slavery (from Genesis. 37) shows us as much about Jacob's bad practices as a parent as it does God's grand design.

Later the reality that we had children at different stages and seasons kicked in. At one point we had children in elementary, middle school and high school all at the same time. (If you feel the need to pray for us, I thank you).

Though that season was difficult, we found that the most important things were addressing what we saw, accepting our children and aiding in their development.

Though he were a Son, yet learned he obedience by the things which he suffered.

Hebrews 5:8

Scripturally, we see that even Christ, as an adolescent needed guidance. This resulted in Him learning obedience.

And he said unto them, How is it that ye sought me? wist ye not that I must be about my Father's business?

And they understood not the saying which he spake unto them.

And he went down with them, and came to Nazareth, and was subject unto them: but his mother kept all these sayings in her heart.

And Jesus increased in wisdom and stature, and in favour with God and man.

Luke 2:49-52

I believe it's these lessons that He was taught early on that aided Him with His destiny to reach and overcome Calvary.

Congratulations. You made it through Parenting 101. But wait, we're not through yet. Welcome to Parenting 102.

CHAPTER THREE: **PARENTING 101**

"Children begin by loving their parents. After time they judge them. Rarely, if ever do they forgive them"

~ Oscar Wilde

CHAPTER FOUR

PARENTING 102
(PARENTING PRE-TEENS 10-12)

Welcome to the time when your children know more than anyone, or shall I say they believe they know more than anyone around them. They may be age ten, but they have been exposed to so much that they have the thought patterns of some a twenty-year-olds from our generation. In their minds, they now meet the criteria or are qualified for responding to, complaining about, emoting and questioning just about all of what we have decided as the parents. The barrage of questions begin, "Why?", "How come?", "Why won't you let me?" just to name a few. They begin hitting us with statements such as, "That's not fair!", "You don't understand me!" and so on and so forth. Then comes the universal comparison to a friend's parent (usually as it pertains to a decision that is way off base). It's at times like these that I like to inform them that they are not Vanna White and I'm not Pat Sajak. This is not Wheel of Fortune or any other game show with options, choices and alternatives. This is me parenting you by way of maturity, responsibility and accountability before God.

Then, as if that's not enough, here comes the onslaught of full blown puberty. Now that thing comes on the scene and they begin receiving new revelations, emotions and hormones and they understandably confuse all these new "developments" with being a grown up. A wise person once told me this, "It takes a lot more than just the parts to make a airplane!" We have to help them understand that using anything for a purpose outside its God ordained purpose amounts to abuse and disorder. Merely having the equipment does not qualify us for the assignment. Having a parachute, but not knowing how to operate it or handle it still equates to you being hurt, injured or even killed with what you needed in your possession. So our priority must be to give them an understanding of who they are internally right in the midst of all that is taking place happening externally.

How they see us seeing them is critical at this stage. Affirming them is essential. We must ensure that we are talking to them, because you can bet your bottom dollar that there are others already in their ear. We must continue to show affection or they will seek and find it from alternative sources. If we withhold our version of love, there are many others out there willing to administer the "street" version. We as parents have to pay close attention to changes in behavior, have conversations with them, press for their thoughts and opinions and then aid them in decisions regarding those matters. I personally believe that this is the greatest time of distraction, attack and diversion for our children with regards to the family union. They must deal with the television, miseducation, music with explicit implications and information as well as a perverted perception of what is right and acceptable in life. Between what's on DVDs, MP3s and the immoral climate at the movie theaters it would almost seem as if there is nowhere for them to turn to. And with the dragnet that we call the internet, it's a tough, 24 hour a day, never let your guard down job being a good parent. If you'll note, I said tough, not impossible. When "Go to your room!", means surfing the internet, watching television, calling, e-mailing, or texting a friend (usually someone with the same level or less conviction) we have a problem. In making these decisions, we must not remove them from us altogether or simply release them into the presence of someone else. We must choose to relate to them and redirect them in a positive but firm manner. All of the aforementioned obstacles can, if properly used and applied, be great tools for them. Not, however, at the price of creating or aiding in family confusion or division. Nor where these tools are given so that we, as parents, can be excused from our roles. We are still responsible for training them, developing them and maturing them into model citizens. In Luke 2:49-52, we see a twelve year old child in the church exploring His own purpose and believing He knows what's best. And even though His name is Jesus, the Son of the Living God, even He during this time had to submit to His parents. His submission releases Him to His time of training and learning in preparation for His earthly ministry. Like Joseph and Mary, we must be committed to training our own children. Training them in the small things such as how to answer someone. That as a mature adult, you do so by speaking and not by nodding or grunting, but with eye to eye contact.and speaking confidently. This also means disciplining them when necessary and not backing off or away from them due to their discomfort. Note; the areas you don't parent in now will most likely hurt you later on in your own assignment.

For I have told him that I will judge his house for ever for the iniquity which he knoweth; because his sons made themselves vile, and he restrained them not.

And therefore I have sworn unto the house of Eli, that the iniquity of Eli's house shall not be purged with sacrifice nor offering for ever.

I Samuel 3:13-14

If we don't restrain them in their process God may very well respond to us. Even complaining must be addressed or they will grow into foot-stomping, teeth-sucking, eye-rolling, neck-gyrating young adults who don't know how to respond toward us or anyone else for that matter. Please understand, God has given you and I the authority to raise our family.

Let every soul be subject unto the higher powers. For there is no power but of God: the powers that be are ordained of God.

Romans 13:1

When God gives authority, He gives His love, His protection, His provision and someone to cover, direct and love you. They have to realize that every time they reject dad and mom, they are really rejecting God's set authority. It's also an important matter that we deal with stubbornness. We have to really let them see what God thinks of it.

For rebellion is as the sin of witchcraft, and stubbornness is as iniquity and idolatry. Because thou hast rejected the word of the LORD, he hath also rejected thee from being king.

I Samuel 15:23

God sees it as the sin of witchcraft. Either we decide to resist and move into rebellion, or we submit to the God given, Spirit led authority of our parents.

PARENTING OUR CHILDREN AS TEENAGERS 13-18

At this point they have reached a time of emphasis on physical appearance and acceptance that is filled with social turbulence. Some of their underlying issues are inferiority, not feeling as though they are good enough, insecurity, or how they believe others see them, and conformity, feeling as though they have to be seen as part of the "in-crowd" socially. They are learning or trying to learn about carrying themselves properly, appreciating and maintaining themselves physically. Their concern now shifts to how they appear or rank relationally and on keeping up with all the "411" (information).

Unfortunately, they don't know what we know, that the folks that are in now are usually out just a little while later. The folks they wish they were "in" with now will be the very same ones they wonder about in about ten years. This is the time of establishing and setting their own convictions, positions and boundaries. And with that being said, they must still learn to live with and love others in spite of their differences. They will either hear the truth from you or have it "revealed" to them by others. If the latter takes place you will get to see the power of influence up close and personal. The areas I'm referring to include but are not limited to smoking, drinking and sexual advancement. They have no clue as to the repercussions of their actions or decisions will have upon them personally or to their friends' lives, bodies and families.

My son, if sinners entice thee, consent thou not.

Proverbs 1:10

It is also at this stage that they need to be reminded that although they think all of their peers know everything under the sun, they don't. They must learn a hard truth; that they themselves don't actually know everyone as well as they have led themselves to believe. Here is your ammunition to help answer when they go into the, "everybody else is going, doing and getting......fill in the blank!" Truth is, everyone may be about 12-20 kids at the most, hardly *everybody*. Remind them that the kids they allow to influence them and give a place of prominence to may seem like the latest and greatest in your neck of the woods, but the city, state and even the county are a whole lot bigger, let alone the world. It is during this hour that they need us the most.

We must do our best to affirm them, celebrate them, instruct them and encourage them. Our goals should be establishing love and authority from 0-10 and then love and influence from 11-18. Hopefully our tactics in leading them are not based on fear; us being bigger, louder or stronger. Rather, we have developed a relationship of trust and understanding.

The goals must not be so harsh and lofty, as to drive them away or toward others, if anything we should drive them inward and upward toward God. Notice how their response changes as ours does. Not

94

when we utilize shouting but when we start influencing. Not by name calling, but influencing, not screaming, but lovingly relating to them and establishing our influence. I often ask my children, "If I gave you a car, would you let one of your friends drive it now?", you see all of their friends are under 15. Of course they say no, then I challenge them to answer me as to why? They tell me that they're not experienced enough, old enough or not wise enough. Then I ambush them with, "Well if they can't drive your car, don't let them drive your life!" To our young men, let's not ask how you can "get with", sleep with or make as many babies as possible, but rather how many babies, families, calamities, injuries, and emotional casualties will you leave in the wake of your selfish, self-gratifying journey. My question to the men is this, "How can you knowingly abuse, misuse and confuse?" Remember, boys play boy games with boy toys, but men commit to one woman, and are known for standing rather than playing.

I beseech you therefore, brethren, by the mercies of God, that ye present your bodies a living sacrifice, holy, acceptable unto God, which is your reasonable service.

And be not conformed to this world: but be ye transformed by the renewing of your mind, that ye may prove what is that good, and acceptable, and perfect, will of God.

Romans 12:1-2

What? know ye not that he which is joined to an harlot is one body? for two, saith he, shall be one flesh.

But he that is joined unto the Lord is one spirit.

Flee fornication. Every sin that a man doeth is without the body; but he that committeth fornication sinneth against his own body.

What? know ye not that your body is the temple of the Holy Ghost which is in you, which ye have of God, and ye are not your own?

For ye are bought with a price: therefore glorify God in your body, and in your spirit, which are God's.

I Corinthians 6:16-20

And fear not them which kill the body, but are not able to kill the soul: but rather fear him which is able to destroy both soul and body in hell.

Matthew 10:28

We need to make sure we have the right kind of fear, that being reverential awe.

The fear of man bringeth a snare: but whoso putteth his trust in the LORD shall be safe.

Proverbs 29:25

If any be blameless, the husband of one wife, having faithful children not accused of riot or unruly.

Titus 1:6

Remind them of the importance of self-control. I tell our youth that the way to spell true physical maturity is V-I-R-G-I-N-I-T-Y. It is demonstrated and manifested in the statement, "I'm waiting until I get married!" Now that is what I call physical responsibility and maturity. Help them develop a healthy sense of self worth. Let them know that they don't need somebody to be validated. Please don't let them buy into that, "If you love me, then you'll let me…" nonsense. God loves me and He showed it as He died for me. That tells me that your boy must love himself more than he loves you. Real love resembles that of Jesus, if he loves her then he'll die to his flesh for her. He won't put undue pressure or stress on her.

If you have already fallen or given in, repent and get back up again in the love and forgiveness of Christ. We must teach them the power of even one sexual encounter. The possible effects derived from that one encounter. One moment of self indulgence can equal out to three different sins, two soul ties, five possible STDs and one possible family (yes, I am talking babies). This one encounter could have a lasting effect on the rest of your life.

Remember parents, they may look like adults on the outside, but they are still developing on the inside. Watch what they watch, listen to their conversations, do surprise room inspections, and don't lead or leave your child out of God's presence (that's right, church!). No matter how old if they are under your roof they will attend church. Note this, that where there is no experience or contact with someone there is no consciousness of that someone. Remember, Godly men come from being influenced by Godly men and Godly women come from being influenced by Godly women. Sheep beget sheep.

Behold, I and the children whom the LORD hath given me are for signs and for wonders in Israel from the LORD of hosts, which dwelleth in mount Zion.

Isaiah 8 :18

Remind your child that it doesn't take a bunch of people to wield great influence. Daniel and the three with him made a great shift in their society. It took one girl named Mary and one boy named Joseph to change the direction of the whole world.

PARENTING OUR CHILDREN AS YOUNG ADULTS 19-22

At this age it's a time of trying, stretching forth, proving and yes even stumbling.

And not many days after the younger son gathered all together, and took his journey into a far country, and there wasted his substance with riotous living.

Luke 15:13

Some of the struggle is due to the fact that they feel like they know all about life (sound familiar). At the same time, they are finding out, in fact, how little they truly know. Now is the time they must answer the hardest questions of their young lives. Where should I go? Where should I live? What is it I should be doing? What is it I really want out of life? Even though they have become this grown person, they very much still need our wisdom, direction, "suggestions" and yes from time to time our financial provision.

Somewhere along in here is "the rub" of being the one seen as the authority or the one allowed to be an influencer in their life choices and decisions. In reality that's why they tend to start dropping by the house and start calling for little to no reason at all; Why they start stopping in, and just checking on you. You see, your home to them will always represent a place of stability and safety for your family. Yes they come and eat the food, but they really need their folks. We have to be available for when, not if they blow it, miss it, or make a mess of it. There is somewhere that they can go to be built back up, where they can breathe easy and be loved.

Eventually they will leave again and come back again and again and maybe even again. They can return as needed, but at some point we have begun to set guidelines and limitations as well as expectations. Our goal is to aid them in getting going again, living again, on their own again. They should always have an open door to come back to their home and our heart. As long as they are with us, we are to keep shaping and developing in them a Christian mindset, encouraging Godly friendships and helping them to develop and discover their gifts and talents as well as strengthen their weaknesses.

When I was a child, I spake as a child, I understood as a child, I thought as a child: but when I became a man, I put away childish things.

I Corinthians 13:11

We should always assist in giving them goals of obtaining their own job, home, money, car, church and place in society. Their independence hinges on this. Our process must be like that of Abraham and Isaac. He prepared him spiritually, positioned him financially, gave him a picture of how to operate relationally and how to love unconditionally.

And she said unto him, My father, if thou hast opened thy mouth unto the LORD, do to me according to that which hath proceeded out of thy mouth;

forasmuch as the LORD hath taken vengeance for thee of thine enemies, even of the children of Ammon.

Judges 11:36

We are to have the same thing that God has for them, it is an expectation and a hope. Maturity is always proved by being willing to take responsibility as well as being able to deal with the consequences of irresponsibility.

And the same man had four daughters, virgins, which did prophesy.

Acts 21:9

PARENTING OUR CHILDREN AS ADULTS 23 & UP

Here we're in the midst of full blown living and moving. These are times of discussing and disagreeing, but in a manner in which both side are still honoring, respecting and appreciating the process of communication.

And both Jesus was called, and his disciples, to the marriage.

And when they wanted wine, the mother of Jesus saith unto him, They have no wine.

Jesus saith unto her, Woman, what have I to do with thee? mine hour is not yet come.

His mother saith unto the servants, Whatsoever he saith unto you, do it.

John 2:2-5

They are learning the art of valuing, considering and reverencing. Developing these things in the form of relationships by keeping them healthy and maintaining them. The key for us as parents is to gain the respect of our children as an adult.

Therefore shall a man leave his father and his mother, and shall cleave unto his wife: and they shall be one flesh.

Genesis 2:24

The end result of good parenting is not just that they live to become a grown up, but that they become our adult friend. We may not see eye to eye on everything, but we can respect one another and even be friends on a certain level. Sometimes we must ask ourselves when dealing with our grown children, "Is this a biblical issue, sin issue or my own opinion?" Learn what's worth fighting for and what's not. Choose your battles wisely. Where things don't line up with you, let them know, but do it in love. Love them and entrust them to the God of the Heavens.

And Ruth said, Intreat me not to leave thee, or to return from following after thee: for whither thou goest, I will go; and where thou lodgest, I will lodge: thy people shall be my people, and thy God my God.

Ruth 1:16

Learn to see them in their own identity. They will, no doubt, become their own man, their own woman. This is where we must bank on all the deposits we have made in them throughout their youthful stages. This is where we call on the harvest of all the seed that we have sown into their lives while they were in our care. We must give space for new relationships. We cannot be controlling, smothering or demanding. You need to go do something. Pick up a hobby. Go golfing, swimming, skiing or biking. Start the next chapter in your life, no matter what God still has more for you. Start a business or travel! Enjoy the fact that you are still young and full of the breath of life.

"Home Work for Parents"

Daily Family Confession - Daily we speak the word of God over our children, to cover them, remind them, release and reinforce in them all that God has for them.

Thou shalt also decree a thing, and it shall be established unto thee: and the light shall shine upon thy ways.

Job 22:28

Saturday Morning - Eating and cleaning. Big breakfast is what we call it, because it's the one day we all sit down and have eggs, bacon, biscuits and fruit as a family. We're not rushed. The cleaning part is chores, begun ten to twenty minutes after breakfast, this teaches them responsibility and respect for where they live and what they've been given.

Vocabulary Money - There are times during the summer, or whenever they aren't in school for that matter, that we intentionally build their vocabulary. We just get words out of the dictionary and post the word and meaning. If they can spell it and know the definition of it from memory, they get paid an extra five bucks. This a way for them to earn extra money while at the same time expand their vocabulary and keep them sharp mentally.

Car Washing/Driver Training - Car washing gets my car clean, creates fun activites that consist of usually getting wet at the end, and create a little time for driver education training for the older ones.

Prayer at Night - This does not take as long as you think, but will have a lasting affect on and in your child. What will they go to sleep thinking about with you reading a chapter of scripture and having each one pray before lights out? This ensures God is on their mind as they sleep. We get to hear their hearts and the Word enters into their life on a nightly basis.

Prayer Powered Car - Our kids know in the mornings during the week, my car doesn't move until one of them prays.

Weekly Family Night - We try hard to keep this regular in some manner, whether it be bowling, eating out, going to the theater or renting movies. It's their night usually, and as they get older they get to choose what we will do. We have five children, so it must be put to a vote, if they can't settle it, we enact our veto power and either myself or their Mom get the final say.

Homework Habits - From their first experience with school train them to come home and find a quiet spot to knock out homework. We are parents of elementary kids, junior high kids and high school kids. We've noticed if you establish this early on, they will carry it through automatically as they grow.

Odd Jobs - This can be a plethora of things such as closets, car interiors, taking the trash out, doing the dishes, washing windows, washing clothes or anything else around the house that needs to be done.

Vacations - We now take them away twice a year, during spring break and in the summer. They are our family vacations (my wife and

I also take our own). This was not always an option, but they need it as much as we do.

Advocating at School - We show up for everything, the good, the bad and the not even totally necessary. We've noticed that the parents that show up are the parents of the children that teachers and staff tend to respect a little, knowing that their adjustment with the children will be responded to.

Extra-curricular Activities - Anytime any of our kids play instrument or sports we already know we are going to make every effort to get them to practice, and show up at every game possible. We also make sure to be one of the loudest people cheering for them. Last year alone we had two basketball players, a volleyball player, a flutist and a choir member. And yes, one of us made it to each performance. It's not easy, but you have to work it.

Birthdays - In our home we have traditions. We'll wake up early and wake everybody in the house so we can all sing happy birthday to the birthday person. Then we either have their favorite meal waiting in the wings or we take them out for it. Cake and ice cream still rank highly in our home with kids of 9, 10, 12, 14 and 15. The smaller ones still get school birthday celebrations on their special day.

Christmas - We are Christians first and family second, meaning Jesus' birthday is first and foremost His day before it is our day. We have instilled the tradition of reading about the birth of Christ and then discussing what we are thankful for. After that we sing happy birthday to Jesus. Then we go and open presents. Our kids were not taught about Santa Clause because we didn't want them to change their behavior for or esteem a man they would never see and not appreciate the parents who are with them daily.

Report Cards - Tradition is that the honor roll equals $20, high honors (3.7 or better) equals $25. At the time of my authoring this book our kids regularly make honor roll. We believe in a real balance of reward and discipline. Our kids have averaged honor roll for most of their school years so far for all of their lives.

Developing Clear Steps of Discipline - 1) a stern talking to 2) sent to your room 3) loss of privileges (i.e. TV, games, outside, sports, etc.) If disrespect or blatant disobedience is the culprit, we go straight to 4) spanking (yeah, I said it. It's in print too!)

Contracts - A pastor friend of mine in Florida Pastor P.C. Cornelius does this. We're not there yet, but in regard to car keys and phones he makes contracts of responsibilities for the kids in his family. Spelled out means of correction, lost privileges and consequences that are preconceived and agreed upon.

Cell Phones - For our home thirteen is the age of opportunity. They get pay as they go. If they can pay, then they can talk. There are times we may help them, but for the most part they are on their own. This helps create responsibility, a work ethic and some creativity as well as initiative.

Three Day - Family days are Mondays, Wednesdays and Fridays. We try to be home in the evenings on three days intentionally to spend time with our family.

Home Phone - We have four girls and one boy (yes, pray for him), but they all know that they have a time limit on the house phone, twenty minutes. After that they can use it later if no one else is on it.

Televisions - In our home, we are out numbered five kids to two parents. There is no way we could effectively govern five to six television sets. So we have two and both are on the first floor in the family room and in the living room. This is done with dual intention. The first is so that we can govern their viewing. If they are watching it, we can see or hear it. The second is that it creates family places, where we watch and enjoy together.

Computer Time - Yes, you guessed it, time limits. Twenty to thirty minutes and it's someone else's turn. The only change is when someone has to do homework, in this scenario they have priority.

CHAPTER FOUR: **PARENTING 102**

"The way I see it, if you want the rainbow, you gotta put with the rain"

~ *Dolly Parton*

CHAPTER FIVE

BLENDED AND A BLESSING

Our world today is filled with many different types of families; some traditional, and some not so traditional due to the various break ups, make ups, decisions and relationships that people have had. One of the increasingly common types are now called blended families. I personally prefer this term over the expressions step, adopted or even broken. The term blended refers to something that has been selected, elected and brought into position to produce a desired combination or result.

One may ask what is it that causes families to be blended. It's a decision to add to or form a new family from either a single parent choosing to marry someone, a parent or parents choosing to adopt, or someone taking responsibility for the death of another family member by raising their children.

Blending and crafting these new families from broken ones brings the risk of a number of issues. But while the problems that may be caused can be critical, I believe the greater concern is this: how do we receive it, adjust for it, process it and get through it? Even though seeing families destroyed just to build something new is not God's intention, God is willing to work in them and bring redemption to every willing person and every condition because His children are in them.

Beloved, every family can be a phenomenal family. Are there blended families in the Bible? Yes. God's man Moses came from a blended home. Esther had one - her uncle raised her. The prophet Samuel was born in one house and raised in another. Joseph was born into the proverbial baby-momma-drama family. Even King Solomon came about from an estranged relationship. Yet God still chose them, called them, used them and blessed them. Even though He blessed them, like all of us, they all grew up in dysfunction because of sin.

What are some of the struggles that tend to manifest in blended families?

- Division
- Rejection
- Separation
- Isolation
- Favoritism

What do the parents need? Parents in these blended and blessed families must walk in real maturity. They must possess a sincere commitment to unity, creating an inseparable alliance. They cannot allow any undermining or child-parent arrangements without both parents' agreement. There can be no private agendas or downing the outside parent. Each adult must work to create respect and common goals.

What do the children need? First and foremost any children need acceptance and attention. They need the assurance of being freed from any guilt over what went wrong in the previous relationships. They need structure. Allow the child to be a child. They need safety and stability. We cannot make them deal with adult decisions or be infected with our own frustrations, thoughts of rejection and issues from hurt and unforgiveness.

What are some of the top issues?

- Agreed Discipline
- The Process for Resolving Conflicts
- The Role of Each Parent
- Clear Responsibilities

I pray that they would never be called a stepfamily, but blended family. Steps are meant to be walked on and stepped on to get from one level to another. That is not God's plan for the lives of His people. We need to stop confusing children with wrong relationships and wrong definitions. Let's stop telling them this is your uncle. Just tell them 'this is mom's friend' or 'daddy's friend'. When we improperly label our relationships to them, we in turn give them a wrong definition of what they should expect from people who rightfully have those labels. If it's good for a corporation to give an employee a 90-day probation period before full employment status is given, then maybe when it comes to this person being apart of your family they might first have to pass the 90-day test. Use this time to know them before they get attached emotionally, financially or physically with you and your children.

My example of a blended family is really as basic as a blended smoothie. It reveals the plan, process and price to be satisfied. It's through a process of buying, being brought and being broken that our family becomes one and brings satisfaction.

BLESSED WHEN EVERYONE BUY'S IN

First we have to realize that all people, like the ingredients of a good smoothie are different. They have and bring their own experiences and processes. But we all have to be willing to be peeled and processed to produce one common thing that is refreshing and fulfilling. We must be willing to sacrifice, give up, give over, give to and discover one another. And like the smoothie, each one brings something and receives something. They don't compete they complete.

Whoever is not willing to work at being a family is the one who will bring about division. Please understand that any house, like any 'kingdom, divided against itself shall not stand' (Matthew. 12:25). No one can have what they want every time they want it. We may want a certain weekend or part of the week to share the kids, be alone, go away, etc. But in order to get some of those things we need to begin with lowering the walls that divide us. The adults should find time to meet to find points of agreement and generate plans and goals that are good for all involved, as well as guidelines for everyone. (This meeting should include all adults only). The discussion should only be on what's best for the child(ren). It should cover how to balance time spent, treasure given, home schedules, vacation times, holidays, weekends, birthday plans, emergency plans, etc. It's work, but your family and the peace it produces are worth it. More importantly, God is for it, and will use it to help, if you let Him.

Let's use these terms:

Residing parent – The one that had custody of the children prior to the relationship. Their responsibility has a lot of the weight on it. Their role is to love the new parent and the child and facilitate the process of blending. It takes managing, balancing, teaching, learning, re-prioritizing and protecting all this. It's very humbling, but rewarding.

Incoming parent – The one who is brought in and put into on-the-job training. Congratulations! You have seen the value of your new spouse. Now learn how to love all of them, which includes their children. It takes adjusting, sharing, balancing, talking, and once again humbling. You'll need patience, growth, and a lot of faith in God and your new spouse. You just went from one family to three different families with a lot of different perceptions and expectations. From the residing parent you might be met with a range of positions and attitudes; some shifting, changing, inspecting, fearing and possibly some intimidating and normal desire to protect their child. In time trust and rest will come. So give it time.

Please don't forget the child(ren). They go through a process of their own. They too are questioning, re-aligning, readjusting, rule changing, losing some exclusivity but gaining in family. They have their own set of fears, moments of doubt and position in the new family to figure out. In reality they go from two sets of family traditions, customs and perceptions to three or more different families all at once. As parents you have to allow some room for them to be open and ask questions; mature ones and immature ones. This helps ease their mental and emotional well being.

We have to be willing to give them what God gives us: unconditional love and grace. We need to offer a load of forgiveness with a healthy heap of longsuffering. Just as the word of God says we have been adopted in Him, and grafted in. So we must do our best in the process of love and acceptance. God's word says "ye were not my people, but are now made my people" and just as we have been accepted in the beloved, we now have to accept another. It's realizing that every child is an extension of the residing parent, and in rejecting the child, we reject a part of our new spouse.

Jesus said if you reject me you reject the one who sent me. To fully receive of this process you have to be willing to pay the full price for it. God intends we step up and have compassion on the children in this situation.

And when she had opened it, she saw the child: and, behold, the babe wept. And she had compassion on him, and said, This is one of the Hebrews' children.

Then said his sister to Pharaoh's daughter, Shall I go and call to thee a nurse of the Hebrew women, that she may nurse the child for thee?

And Pharaoh's daughter said to her, Go. And the maid went and called the child's mother.

And Pharaoh's daughter said unto her, Take this child away, and nurse it for me, and I will give thee thy wages. And the women took the child, and nursed it.

Exodus 2:6-9

Note: this is the Pharaoh's daughter and she does it without the Word of God or the Holy Spirit in her) that compassion begins emotionally. His compassion must be given to each person and the goal is to receive every as our own.

And he brought up Hadassah, that is, Esther, his uncle's daughter: for she had neither father nor mother, and the maid was fair and beautiful; whom Mordecai, when her father and mother were dead, took for his own daughter.

Esther 2:7

And Elkanah her husband said unto her, Do what seemeth thee good; tarry until thou have weaned him; only the LORD establish his word. So the woman abode, and gave her son suck until she weaned him.

I Samuel 1:23

BLESSED WHEN EVERYONE IS BROUGHT INTO THE PLAN

Much like the fruit, we need to be free of old wounds, spoiled spots and open sores. They might be wrong mindsets, old mindsets, unclosed issues, financial matters, disagreements, or unforgiveness, bitterness etc. Just as every piece of the smoothie must be skinned and re-positioned and brought into unison, we must also be prepared.

Each parent now has to focus on what's best for the children, the family as a whole and how to get everyone to a point of agreement. Real questions need to be dealt with, such as: What are each parent's fears, thoughts or apprehensions; what are our stated positions on correction, celebrations, provision and discipline; what are comfortable limitations, expectations and degrees of participation in regard to parental responsibilities?

Remember, communication removes questions and information nullifies confusion. This first process is for adults, then we bring in the children. Remember all good smoothies are usually made with a little spill here and there. There will be bumps along the road. Be patient with it.

The process continues with each fruit being dropped in a bowl whole. Then each one goes through the blender. The turning and gyrating of life situations and unplanned conditions one by one begin changing, breaking, and re-molding them into one. The truth is unless you become broken you won't benefit. Unless you submit to the mixing you are the one delaying the whole process. There will be areas you must change in order to become one. You've got to stop resisting, and fighting and warring and start yielding to what God is doing and making through you and your family. Believe it or not Jesus knows all too well about this process. He himself went through it.

Then Joseph being raised from sleep did as the angel of the Lord had bidden him, and took unto him his wife:

And knew her not till she had brought forth her firstborn son: and he called his name JESUS.

Matthew 1:24-25

He bought into it, then he was brought into the plan God had for him.

In this process we have to be willing to accept change to us, in us and through us.

And Mary said, Behold the handmaid of the Lord; be it unto me according to thy word. And the angel departed from her.

Luke 1:38

Our acceptance equals agreement. 'This is my family. Even though this might not be my biological child, this is my child. This is my family and my destiny.

Then said his sister to Pharaoh's daughter, Shall I go and call to thee a nurse of the Hebrew women, that she may nurse the child for thee?

And Pharaoh's daughter said to her, Go. And the maid went and called the child's mother.

And Pharaoh's daughter said unto her, Take this child away, and nurse it for me, and I will give thee thy wages. And the women took the child, and nursed it.

Exodus 2:7-9

Following this model also means that we work in agreement to keep accountability.

And Mordecai walked every day before the court of the women's house, to know how Esther did, and what should become of her.

Esther 2:11

Each parent has to be willing to accept and take responsibility.

And Eli blessed Elkanah and his wife, and said, The LORD give thee seed of this woman for the loan which is lent to the LORD. And they went unto their own home.

And the LORD visited Hannah, so that she conceived, and bare three sons and two daughters. And the child Samuel grew before the LORD.

I Samuel 2:20-21

BLESSED WHEN EVERYONE SUBMITS TO THE BREAKING PROCESS

The process of blending is sometimes loud. At times it's fast and shaking and riveting. Most of the time it's a little messy. But remember, in the end it will be satisfying, refreshing and rewarding. Much like the smoothie mixing process in the mall, we don't control it. It's an example of God interrupting us, like a company relocating us, or someone leaving us because their feelings, thoughts and emotions changed. The process is challenging but the incoming parent must know how to slice time, expectations, and decisions into threes. The residing parent-has to aid in pulling off protective devices, and pulling down defenses, the remaining parent has to carve out and find out new limits, time restraints and what's a good distance without being indifferent. It takes some yielding, submitting, and some slow stirring to get the best mix.

The process of blending will take time, but it's well worth the wait and the work. You must be willing, naturally, emotionally, financially, relationally and parentally. All must be willing to adjust and give some level of affection, attention, respect and appreciation. It will take accepting and thinking like Joseph *Then Joseph her husband, being a just man, and not willing to make her a public example, was minded to put her away privily* (Matthew 1:19) to be successful.

Blending breaks into our own plans both publicly and personally, so we need to be prepared to follow after God, and follow after love even when its inconvenient. *And the angel answering said unto him, I am Gabriel, that stand in the presence of God; and am sent to speak unto thee, and to shew thee these glad tidings. And when she saw him, she was troubled at his saying, and cast in her mind what manner of salutation this should be.* (Luke 1:19, Luke 1:29).

BLESSED WHEN EVERYONE SEES THE VALUE OF BLENDING

For the success of any blended family it is critically important that the adults share the same goal. When the common goal is unifying and not side taking, territory taking or self protection, then there really is hope for a happy and productive family unit. That's when we can respect everyone's identity, value each other's diversity and choose to operate respectfully. In the end, each part is necessary to produce a refreshing, reviving, and restoring family.

Like anything else, the more you pour in the more you receive out. The more you put in the greater the value. Just remember that the goal is for all to become one. Believe it or not all families have some form of blend, even if just the two become one. The goal is the same naturally and spiritually. We are to pursue unity, oneness and nothing less.

And the child grew, and she brought him unto Pharaoh's daughter, and he became her son. And she called his name Moses: and she said, Because I drew him out of the water.

Exodus 2:10

The people listening to this momentous event understood his value from the natural house but not the spiritual house. They knew Christ only as Joseph's son. They did not understand that He grew up with more than one perception of Himself – with double confirmation of his person. Both of His fathers spoke to him, visited him, were proud of him, cared for him, provided for him. Christ became a picture of both of them –the expressed image of God.

And now I am no more in the world, but these are in the world, and I come to thee. Holy Father, keep through thine own name those whom thou hast given me, that they may be one, as we are.

John 17:11

"Homework for Blended Families"
- Am I willing to Blend?
- Am I willing to change for my new family?
- Am I willing to be broken to be crafted into the person that will be best for this family?
- Will we set up meetings with the other parents?
- Will we draw out limits, and arrangements?
- Will I do my part in this process?

- What is my part?(Incoming, Remaining, or Residing)?
- How will we deal with, vacations, school functions, holidays, birthdays, emergencies, sporting events?
- Have we had any adult meetings or talks privately?
- What's going to be my role?
- Am willing to take it?
- How can we help the child in this process?
- Am I willing to change to create relationships that satisfy?

"Success is more a function of common sense than its is of genius."

~ Ann Wang

CHAPTER SIX

SUCCESSFUL SINGLES

THE PRIORITY OF PREPARATION

There are many different types of singles; those preparing to make moves, those standing still, those desiring and those not even ambitious enough to prepare or plan. Those who are preparing are those positioning themselves, working, saving, living and progressing through life. They refuse to wait for someone to come along and bring life to them. Those singles standing still are those who want a mate, but not badly enough that they're willing to lower their standards just to be with somebody. Usually if you lower your standards too much all you will get is *somebody*. The third type is a person that is single and spends his or her life sleeping, breathing, eating and thinking for hours on end dreaming and day dreaming about meeting, joining, and connecting with someone, anyone for that matter. This is a person who is surely without mastery in the area of singleness.

As a single you operate in preparation. This means not looking for Mr./Ms. Right, but rather becoming Ms/Ms. Right in and of yourself. You must put yourself in a place where you are truly single (meaning separate, unique, complete and whole) all by yourself, with just you and Jesus. Mature singles choose to enjoy their time in singleness and use it productively as not to waste or regret it. Truth be told, the more time you spend trying to find someone the less time you spend enjoying your time in that season. Typically this season becomes a distraction and a frustration rather than a time of celebration to appreciate your freedom.

See Adam wasn't lonely in the garden, he was merely alone. What Adam understood is what we need to understand; that who he was spiritually, personally and socially was determined far prior to him becoming relational. So his worth and value as a person was never based on him being with, connecting to or being hooked up with another person. He was content in his given assignment. Discontentment drives us to an unhealthy and unbalanced need for attachment or involvement. Usually this entails people who may not even be tied to our assignment in this life. How do I know this? See Eve and the Devil in Genesis. Discontentment would indicate that there is a negative aspect, or perception of my position or person, which in turn creates a need to add someone or something. If you are not content with you, remember this; in multiplication zero times anything equals zero.

The questions begin with you. Before you try to go out and find someone to love you, ask yourself if you love you? Before you start liking someone else, do you like you? Are you confident in whom you are? The question is where are you? Are you hunting, chasing, pursuing, and experimenting in the art of changing someone into "the right one". Are you the relationship scientist? While experiments are exciting they are known for being volatile and unpredictable, for exploding, hurting and wounding. Say it with me, "Step away from the white jacket and put down the beaker and goggles." Do it before you cause yourself too much trouble. Those who continue on will end up in situations of pain and suffering, virtually guaranteed to end up violating and hindering Gods timing and possibly reducing their future level of living. Being single is not just waiting, but preparing, standing, growing and evolving into your purpose and eventually into a relationship. The following sections will will offer some help as to some areas and ideas you can work while you wait.

SINGLES MUST DISCOVER GOD'S PLAN FOR THEMSELVES

Understand that if you find a significant other before you know what God desires for you, you will have a person but no purpose and you will not be satisfied. With all the time you have while you are single, you are able to try things and go places all while in the process of finding your purpose. Know this as well, life is not a Jerry Maguire movie ("You complete me..."). Your completion is not found in another person. Rather it was established in creation, and fulfilled through salvation. The first thing we need to know is who we are and whose we are, and we must know that without anyone else in the equation. We can't complete ourselves in and through others, and many times as Christians we have bought into the lie of the world that we can't be happy as a single. Or if you are alone something is wrong with you. Please note that it was God that made man alone and then gave him a place alone, provision alone, a job alone, opportunity alone and responsibility alone before he gave him anybody to share it with.

And the LORD God formed man of the dust of the ground, and breathed into his nostrils the breath of life; and man became a living soul.

And the LORD God planted a garden eastward in Eden; and there he put the man whom he had formed.

And out of the ground made the LORD God to grow every tree that is pleasant to the sight, and good for food; the tree of life also in the midst of the garden, and the tree of knowledge of good and evil.

And a river went out of Eden to water the garden; and from thence it was parted, and became into four heads.

The name of the first is Pison: that is it which compasseth the whole land of Havilah, where there is gold;

And the gold of that land is good: there is bdellium and the onyx stone.

And the name of the second river is Gihon: the same is it that compasseth the whole land of Ethiopia.

And the name of the third river is Hiddekel: that is it which goeth toward the east of Assyria. And the fourth river is Euphrates.

And the LORD God took the man, and put him into the garden of Eden to dress it and to keep it.

And the LORD God commanded the man, saying, Of every tree of the garden thou mayest freely eat:

But of the tree of the knowledge of good and evil, thou shalt not eat of it: for in the day that thou eatest thereof thou shalt surely die.

And the LORD God said, It is not good that the man should be alone; I will make him an help meet for him.

And out of the ground the LORD God formed every beast of the field, and every fowl of the air; and brought them unto Adam to see what he would call them: and whatsoever Adam called every living creature, that was the name thereof.

And Adam gave names to all cattle, and to the fowl of the air, and to every beast of the field; but for Adam there was not found an help meet for him.

Genesis 2:7-20

If you buy into this you will try to make up for what you believe you are missing. Many times singles are competing for and not developing relationships. Some even attempt to become popular or gain status through another person, and oh by the way, yes this is considered using them. Being single means a lot more than, "I'm available". It should mean, "I'm capable, wonderful, purposeful, beautiful and spiritual and all that was before I connected with you." You're someone in completion because of Christ and His kingdom.

And ye are complete in him, which is the head of all principality and power:

Colossians 2:10

It's knowing that you are fearfully and wonderfully made. Even the picture we're given in the Garden of Eden allows us to see that a woman was made to have an identity, live independent or interdependent alongside man.

And the rib, which the LORD God had taken from man, made he a woman, and brought her unto the man.

Genesis 2:22

As well as the man having, operating and living independent and interdependent of woman. Both of them have a relationship with God separate from one another. They had time with God alone, were led by God alone, were in submission to Him alone, and were bought by him alone. What you both want is this a man or a woman in touch with the God of heaven before they try to have a relationship with you. Believe me ladies, you want a man shaped by God, led by God and formed by God. will be well worth the wait.

And the LORD God formed man of the dust of the ground, and breathed into his nostrils the breath of life; and man became a living soul.

Genesis 2:7

And so is that woman of virtue that is developed by God, led by God and guided by the hand of God.

SINGLES MUST DISCERN PEOPLE COMING INTO THEIR WORLD

To discern people is not as hard as we make it out to be, the problem starts when we are desperate. Our wanting and longing causes us to take shortcuts regarding our discernment. Stop dating folks for experimental purposes (just seeing what will happen). Experimenting is taking two different things and making them one by either force or combustion. Stop running out on dates to get rid of the lonely feeling. It's better to feel it than to force something. Stay away from "pity dating". Be careful pity doesn't lead you into the pitter-patter of parenting. First you have to parent the immature significant other, and then if you aren't guarding yourself, you're bringing new lives into the pity party. Or even worse a serial dater, a bug-a-boo or a stalker.

Stop dating "off the radar". They were nowhere in your line of sight before tonight. Let's get rid of "close enough" dating. Close enough equals never enough. In some scenarios you've been hurt by your hope, because you knew who they were and went anyway, hoping to be wrong. Stop dating way below your level, you'll be carrying that relationship for the rest of your life. Get and keep some quality control. You need a couple real friends, maybe your mama and daddy, their mama or daddy, your church leadership, a cop, the FBI (just kidding). Realize that if they don't know God they can't give you God's kind of love. If you have to talk yourself into it, God probably is not in it.

Only date possible marriage material, why frustrate yourself? Save yourself a lot of trouble, hurt and heartache. Don't lower your standards. Get some guidelines (i.e. 1-5 dates, wait on kissing, you don't know where this persons lips have been, or where their hands have been for that matter). Make a plan of personal limits, space in regards to the physical process (i.e. holding hands, hugging), Listen, if most corporations have a 90 day probationary period before you get to join in or experience "benefits"(touch, kiss, etc.) then why shouldn't you. You are a child of the King with purpose and destiny on the inside. Believe me by then you'll know his/her true motivation, whether it's for your money, body, comforts you provide for them personally or whether this is someone who has come into your life for the long haul.

MORE ON DISCOVERING GOD'S PLAN (WILL) FOR YOU

Again, rather than focusing on relating, emoting and searching for someone, use this time to become someone (to become the one). Please realize your completion is not, I repeat, not in another person on the earth. In God you and I were completed in Jesus before the foundation of the earth. It was all done in the Son of God, Jesus the Christ and fulfilled through salvation in Him.

And ye are complete in him, which is the head of all principality and power:

Colossians 2:10

The first thing you have to know is who you are and whose you are. This is rooted in Jesus not any other man or woman. Don't buy into the lie of the world that it takes someone else to complete us, or that you need anyone else to validate you. Here's the proof, when you were born didn't you need to be cut off from someone. This shows that in order for you to be the person of God's intention, you need a level of solitude and your own separate identity as an individual. Once you were separated, did your breathing, living, growing, changing or thinking depend on someone else? I said that to say this, if you are reading this you are still breathing, living, growing, changing, thinking and that is not dependant on someone else. You being happy is not dependant on you being with or without somebody. Nor is something wrong with you if you are not "hooked up" with someone. These are lies the enemy tells you and me to cause us to "hook up" with others who don't have a clue about who we are or our purpose. They don't even know who they are most of the time or have an inkling of their purpose.

We tend to find, and define ourselves by the world's concepts, and not the identity we have been given in Christ Jesus. Sometimes it can become a manipulative situation, where we become willing to use a person to gain a particular status. Or maybe we do it to prove our ability, be accepted socially, fulfill our physical desires, or just so that we're not lonely. These are the most selfish and self-centered reasons for being with a person. Please don't confuse being single with being lonely. In reality the more you focus on loneliness, the more you will be depressed. To be single actually means to be unique, separate, and whole. I reiterate single does not mean available, it means personally able, capable, purposeful, beautiful and spiritual. As we said earlier you are created by God, fearfully and wonderfully made.

I will praise thee; for I am fearfully and wonderfully made: marvellous are thy works; and that my soul knoweth right well.

My substance was not hid from thee, when I was made in secret, and curiously wrought in the lowest parts of the earth.

Psalm 139:14-15

Completion was a decision made from creation and is confirmed in and through the walking out of my salvation. Please remember in the Garden that man was made without the presence or assistance of a woman. Understand the woman was made through a process in which God rendered man unconscious, so he couldn't take any credit in it or for it.

And the rib, which the LORD God had taken from man, made he a woman, and brought her unto the man.

Genesis 2:22

And the LORD God formed man of the dust of the ground, and breathed into his nostrils the breath of life; and man became a living soul.

And the LORD God planted a garden eastward in Eden; and there he put the man whom he had formed.

Genesis 2:7-8

Both demonstrations in creation prove that you are a whole person with or without another person. Please know that we will always be aided, supported, encouraged and loved by other people. However, they come to maybe enhance you, not to ordain you or set you apart. They help develop you, but they didn't design you. This means you were meant to live outside of another or with another but never based on another. Our lives are not determined by our connection, physical expressions, relationship or position with another. See like Eve, you were on the mind of God way before you were on the mind of any other person. God created you to be His woman first before you ever become somebody's girl, anybody's wife, or even a mother. He created us to be His man before we ever become somebody's boy, anybody's boo, or even a daddy. God defines you spiritually, individually, and personally. You are not defined by who are with relationally. It's also how you can check whom you are dating, are they relating to God personally or privately? Does God lead them? Do they hear God? Do they fellowship with God? Where's their garden (church) where they meet Him? Do they have a history of being with God without you? Is God leading him or is she in submission to God? Do they walk with God in your absence? Does he have job (garden), a place to live? Is he subject to accountability? Is he really like Adam or is she really like Eve?

MORE ON DISCERNING THE PEOPLE COMING INTO YOUR LIFE

Be ye not unequally yoked together with unbelievers: for what fellowship hath righteousness with unrighteousness? and what communion hath light with darkness?

And what concord hath Christ with Belial? or what part hath he that believeth with an infidel?

And what agreement hath the temple of God with idols? for ye are the temple of the living God; as God hath said, I will dwell in them, and walk in them; and I will be their God, and they shall be my people.

Wherefore come out from among them, and be ye separate, saith the Lord, and touch not the unclean thing; and I will receive you.

II Corinthians 6:14-17

Discern. Not certain, uncertain? Make certain. Don't allow relationships to continue developing and growing if you are uncomfortable with it as it stands. Have a red flag in your spirit, or uneasiness about it? Better to slow down now than to breakdown later. Just like cars there are certain signs along the road that give insight as to upcoming troubles or hazards. Our infatuation and emotions (especially when tied to physical connections) tend to blur or completely blind our vision and discernment in situations such as these. Like the low fuel light, relationships with low standards can and will leave you stranded.

Make sure to take a look at the check engine light to check their motivation and direction or you can easily end up in a place of stagnation. Low oil light amounts to a lack of spiritual insight. No

Word and no worship equals no will to go after God. If you seem to be seeing an image, but can't quite make it out, be very careful. What looks like a high-speed jet cruising by is really just a buzzard off in the distance. Everything that looks like, sounds like and seems like a plane may not be, it may not be a plane but a real pain. They tend to be what I call a wanna be or a trying to be, with a goal of robbing us of time, energy or destiny.

To be unequally yoked means to be unequally matched up, connected, attached to or in agreement with. The picture is of a wagon pulled by an ox and a dog hooked up to the same yoke or straps. Clearly they don't have the same mind, strength, ways, will or wants. The end result is that the ox drags the dog all over the place, causing pain and inflicting wounds in the process. Ultimately neither fulfills the purpose of producing crops or fruit. Both parties end up busted, disgusted and frustrated due to an unequal attachment that hinder the assignment, goal and purpose. So it is with men and women in faulty and unequal relationships. Unequal can mean being unequal in spiritual understanding, morality, beliefs, life direction or personal decisions. It can also be manifested in the areas of private perceptions, selfish positions, financial provision, unspoken expectations and life vision.

These fundamental inequalities inevitably cross over to other critical arenas such as financial, parental, personal, relational, physical, sexual and views of social issues. Again, nothing beats a good quality control for your life. Have standards, and if they are not marriage material they shouldn't be dating material. They won't change because of how wonderful you are, and they surely won't change because of a ring on their finger. If God hasn't worked on them yet, you don't have all day to wait. You can save yourself a lot of time and emotional pain. Discern them on the approach.

WHAT'S YOUR SINGLE STATUS

Six Types of Single Men
1. *The Player*

Underneath it all he is a self-lover and a user,abuser and mis-user of women. He is only about his own satisfaction.

2. *Pretender*

He tells her and promises her anything to be around her. He'll string her along and tell her he loves her, is going to marry her or whatever he needs to, but never has any intention of marrying her.

3. *Part-Timer*

He's part time in the Word, part time in the world. Typically unstable, incapable of commitment.

4. *Hustler*

He's in it to get it, and that's it. Once gets what he wants, he's gone. He only wants money, your body, somebody to take care of him or do for him. He is not interested in anything else but satisfying himself personally.

5. *Self-Believer*

It's all about him, whether you are with him or not. It's all about what he gets or wants. In his eyes he is the reason he exists. He is God's gift to the world in and of himself..

6. *God Pleaser*

His only goal is to honor God, live for God and have everything in his life glorify God. He desires to do this privately, publicly, financially and relationally in all that he does. He lives in God's presence and God is his reference point.

SIX TYPES OF SINGLE WOMEN
(Some are a review from earlier)
1. *Hoochie*

Everything in her world revolves around her. She uses what she has physically, unconcerned about her self spiritually or mentally, and is totally desensitized to any long term repercussions relationally

2. *Holla Back Girl*

She is in it for what she can get out of it. She embodies the "what have you done for me lately" mentality. If she can't get what she needs, she will leave and "holla back!"

3. *Half-Timer*

She is midway in between the world and the Word of God. She may be holy on certain days in certain ways, but a hell-raiser at other times. She likely has the ability to fool some on Sunday, but will live like the world every other day.

4. *Ms. Desperate*

This woman will allow herself to be abused, misused and used. She is willing to sacrifice time, money, family, dignity and body for the love of somebody or anybody for that matter.

5. *The Bitter*

Since this woman has been heartbroken, wounded, hurt, and left out in the cold, she has determined not to ever let that happen again. Her bitterness keeps her in loneliness and repels those that would help bring her restoration.

6. *Holy Woman*

This is a woman with strong convictions. She lives and operates from a spiritual position of authority. She makes Godly decisions, and has a high standard for every relationship that she enters into. She is known for her focus on Jesus.

My brothers and sisters, where do you fit in this matrix? What do you want to be? What will you choose to be? Who do you want to be linked to? Discern them and make decisions based on what God shows you. Are they dateable, marriage material? Are they spiritual, carnal, traditional, social, or just plum loco? Are they a giver, intercessor, worshipper, follower, leader, or wanderer? Are you like Samson or the woman by the well, so relationally starved that you don't mind personal injury, lost of destiny, or being hindered in your own spiritual intimacy? Remember the stages in a natural relationship; these are typical but may vary depending on maturity level.

- 3-5 months = infatuation, "Here we get our butterflies and longing and that awkwardness that comes from meeting someone new that you really like where there's a potential for a real relationship.
- 6-9 months = celebration

This stage could enter into passion. Then emotions enter in with rose colored glasses on. Usually soon thereafter the real person starts to come out.

- 10-12 months= realization

Now the real person starts to slip out. Do you really know them or should you hand them the Oscar? At this point even if they come out, will you be addicted to drama (you know, my TNT brothers or sisters, you just love drama).

MAKE PREPARATION BY DEVELOPING YOUR OWN PERSON

What are you doing with the time God is currently giving you? Have you taken personal inventory lately? Where are you? How are you managing you physically, spiritually, emotionally, mentally and socially? Are you *becoming* the right person, rather than *looking* for the right person? Is your stock up? Would you be an asset or a liability to somebody if God saw fit to bring them to you?

Remember, the kind of fish you catch always depends on the kind of bait you use. Stop seeking and spend some time increasing, building and progressing yourself. How do you view you? How do you view what you do? Are you doing something you've been wanting and waiting to do? Physically, you have the responsibility for your own body. The truth is - it's God's body.

Some of us need to submit to the Holy Spirit concerning some home improvements. Maybe even an extreme home makeover. You know the singles in the Bible would put a lot of us to shame. Take a sister named Dorcas. She was a business owner, worshipper and a serious believer. She was a Martha Stewart type Christian in her season. The ladies in Luke 8:3, made a difference with there substance in the ministry of Jesus. Mary Magdalene might have had her demons but by the end of the day, she had the benjamins and sowed them gladly into the Kingdom. Then there's Boaz, a brother who was spiritually and socially in tune, while running the business with Kingdom purpose. He had land, crops, and staff. What about Joseph, a single brother rejected by his family, sold to another country. He worked his way up into good positions because God was with him. Brother man was successful *wherever God put him* - even to the point where he eventually ran Pharaoh's kingdom. Adam was already serving God in the garden before God brought him a woman.

Sometimes God wants to see if you would be faithful without before He releases someone to you. Keep in mind relating means serving, submitting, yielding and sometimes even changing. God didn't start bringing about wives until the men were serving Him. Moses was serving Jethro before he married Zipporah. Ruth was serving Naomi before Boaz came.

God's plan is that we get consumed in living, serving and honoring Him and He will do the bringing. Watch what happens when you sell out for the Kingdom of God. In the midst, watch out, the devil will try to send diversions and distractions for your delay and destruction, as well as to humiliate you as a person. Just ask the man named Samson. They are sent to push you into making bad decisions and lead you into erroneous positions.

But I would have you without carefulness. He that is unmarried careth for the things that belong to the Lord, how he may please the Lord:

There is difference also between a wife and a virgin. The unmarried woman careth for the things of the Lord, that she may be holy both in body and in spirit: but she that is married careth for the things of the world, how she may please her husband.

And this I speak for your own profit; not that I may cast a snare upon you, but for that which is comely, and that ye may attend upon the Lord without distraction.

I Corinthians 7:32,34-35

And lo a voice from heaven, saying, This is my beloved Son, in whom I am well pleased.

Matthew 3:17

Get prepared by making your mind, spirit and body ready, as well as your money, career, lifestyle and ideas ready for the introduction of God's chosen into your life.

"Home Work for Single Folk"

<u>Conduct a self-check:</u>
- Is this person marital material?
- Are you engaging in "pity" dates?
- How are you preparing yourself?
- How are you discerning the people coming into your life?
- What kind of single man am I?
- Which of our single woman profiles do I fit?
- Am I committed to giving the people I'm dating at least a 90-day probation period?
- Who is the quality control team in your life?
- Are you in agreement with **Colossians 2:10**?
- Is he Adam?
- Is she Eve?
- Would you be an asset or a liability to somebody?

<u>To Do Lists:</u>
- **Before the Ring List** - What you want to complete/accomplish before marriage!
- **Goals Sheet (2yrs, 5yrs, 10yrs)** - spiritually, financally, relationally, etc. **Proverbs 29:18**
- **Plans to Produce** - What could you make better with your hands? What frustrates you most? What do you hate? What arenas do you struggle with?
- **Steps / Planning** - What do you want to do? When do you want to have it done? What is the start date? Write it down, hang it up, work at it! Those who fail to plan, plan to fail.

- **Travel** - New York, Florida, Caribbean, Spain, London, France, Italy, the Turks and Caucus, Bahamas, Jamaica etc. Where do you want to go?
- **Mentoring** - Who's under you that could benefit from you, your wisdom, your guidance, your direction etc.? Who do you draw from?
- **Invest** - Are you investing time, talents or treasure somewhere, somehow?
- **Live & Enjoy Life** - Celebrate birthdays, holidays and other times with family as often as possible.
- **Start A Business** - What do you like, buy, need, enjoy doing? What do you like working at or with?
- **Buy that Car** - It's an investment and a need. It gives you access and independence.
- **Get an Apartment** - Begin learning to live like an adult. Responsibility brings freedom.
- **Buy the House** - Your net worth and financial opportunities grow as it gains equity and if you get married, you can always sell it and reap the benefits.
- **Take the Test Drive** - Get out and drive the car or cars of your dreams. Try out that motorcycle, ATV,etc.
- **Water Ski** - Get on a jet ski (Just-Ski) Take a trip to the mountains! Get out there and go see the world!

CHAPTER SIX: **SUCCESSFUL SINGLES**

"All progress is hindsight forward."

~ *C.E.S.*

CHAPTER SEVEN

SINGLE PLUS: FORTY OR FIFTY, SIXTY SOME-THING

You must realize that you really are something, and someone special. This time in your life translates into you being more seasoned now, you're matured (good and grown) and your life's trademark should be adding to others, lending support, expanding vision and enjoying life in general. There are some of you that have suffered through, stood through, battled through, and processed through rough relationships; some have even made it through raising children (sometimes grandchildren), all the while dealing and struggling with former husbands. Some of you have dealt with changing vocations, and even managed some of the physical changes that set in during this season. Beloved this is not a time for regretting, replaying, reviewing and rehearsing all the bad things, old things or painful things.

Therefore if any man be in Christ, he is a new creature: old things are passed away; behold, all things are become new.

II Corinthians 5:17

Actually this could be a time of new beginnings, refocusing, reprioritizing or releasing. This is a time for realizing the dreams and celebrating the fact that you are still alive and packed with purpose and destiny. This could be a time for traveling, empty nesting, investing, grand parenting, or a season of financial preparation or increased liberty and freedom. Consider this biblical line of thought, God never mentions anything about retirement, we are always moving towards destiny and serving the kingdom.

Remember, single means being separate, unique and whole. The question is, are you killing time, waiting time or are you using time, maximizing your opportunities in God? Who or what are you adding to? Who or what are you supporting? Who or what are you expanding? Is it your family, ministry or your social status? To who or to what are you lending all of the wisdom, perspective and vision you have acquired? Are you enjoying this time in your life? Will you use it selfishly, or will your life affect & impact others far beyond you? Are you just trying to find the right person or become the right person; all the while living in frustration? Or are you serving and enjoying your current position.

If you are not content with yourself or in love with yourself, then you will never be confident in who you are. It won't matter who God brings your way if you are bound and consumed in what's wrong with you. Personally I do not accept and agree with this "mid-life crisis" nonsense. I believe it's got a lot more to do with us not being submitted to the Christ that dwells in us. We ought not get into making excuses to appease our flesh anytime it takes us outside of our relationship with Christ. Throughout life's changes, we still have to be willing to change, finding our self is still wrought in denying and/or losing ourselves for Jesus. None of our maturation is ever an excuse for not behaving and living in a way that is God-honoring. Age, older age even, never alters God's order or kingdom thought or the standards He holds us to. We will either be an anatomically older us that is just as rebellious or an older us that is still effective and fruitful for the kingdom of God.

The righteous shall flourish like the palm tree: he shall grow like a cedar in Lebanon.

Those that be planted in the house of the LORD shall flourish in the courts of our God.

They shall still bring forth fruit in old age; they shall be fat and flourishing;

Psalm 92:12-14

When we look to our biblical ancestors, the older they got, the more affective they became. Look at the life of Moses, the life of Daniel, the life of Naomi, or Elizabeth; all of them were mature yet still fulfilling God's purpose. While they were still living they continued adding, expanding, supporting or advancing the people, plan and purposes of God. They were still learning, growing, leading and enjoying everyday they had. They were enjoying themselves and giving life to someone else. They were expanding their scope through serving. They were advancing by continual growth in Him and adding to their repertoire by leading and enjoying their livelihood. None of them were focused on their marital status or their lives winding down. Their focus was on fulfilling and finishing everything God *continued* speaking and expecting. That's where we miss it, God doesn't stop speaking destiny and purpose to your life once you hit 40 years old. Let us look with expectancy to what God desires of us when we are 40, 50 or 60 something.

ADDING SOMETHING BY MENTORING

Sometime, usually around forty years of age, a reality starts to kick in. This reality is that we don't know everything, haven't been everywhere and maybe haven't imparted into any other person the very life lessons we wish we'd been given. Mentoring is the opportunity to position the next generation of men and women for kingdom loving, living and advancing. Mentoring is not about how old you are but how willing, giving and sober-minded you are with regards to someone else's future. It presents us with a way to leave *Godly influence*, not just *natural affluence*. It positions us to release an influence that leaves a difference on our world spiritually, mentally, relationally and financially. It's more valuable than material substance that can be lost, it is a spiritual substance that will help them go the distance and accomplish all they desire to in their lives.

In this season we have control over our own freedoms. These freedoms are the freedom of time, talents and if handled properly, treasure. This is the season of being, not performing. We can't just tell kids to be quiet because we are older, bigger or stronger than they are. We cannot tell them to say things and do things, not lead the way ourselves. This is a "do as I say, not as I do" mindset. That is not mentorship. We have to be mature enough to stop with the "it's all about me" attitude, otherwise we might be showing our immaturity.

Are you one that inspires respect, reverence for God and that of your own presence? Does our walk move others to want to know God, or even to worship Him? Do you demonstrate self-restraint and self-control over your passions, decisions and vision? Are you focused on your biological clock ticking away or are you serving? What legacy you are leaving? One way to secure a legacy in the earth is through mentoring, adding, aiding, and advancing someone else. Please, whatever you do, don't be forty going on twenty, or fifty trying to relive your thirties. Just be holy as He is holy.

While they behold your chaste conversation coupled with fear.

Whose adorning let it not be that outward adorning of plaiting the hair, and of wearing of gold, or of putting on of apparel;

But let it be the hidden man of the heart, in that which is not corruptible, even the ornament of a meek and quiet spirit, which is in the sight of God of great price.

1 Peter 3:2-4

Put the skirt down and button the shirt up, this goes for both my men and my women of God. One great way to refrain from getting into others business unnecessarily is to live your life on purpose.

That the aged men be sober, grave, temperate, sound in faith, in charity, in patience. The aged women likewise, that they be in behaviour as becometh holiness, not false accusers, not given to much wine, teachers of good things.

Titus 2:2-3

Brother Saul, the Lord, even Jesus, that appeared unto thee in the way as thou camest, hath sent me, that thou mightest receive thy sight, and be filled with the Holy Ghost.

Acts 9:17

Mentoring could assist you in this. Mentoring has a history of bringing people into maturity and thrusting them towards destiny. *See Ruth and Naomi.*

Then she arose with her daughters in law, that she might return from the country of Moab: for she had heard in the country of Moab how that the LORD had visited his people in giving them bread.

Wherefore she went forth out of the place where she was, and her two daughters in law with her; and they went on the way to return unto the land of Judah.

And Naomi said unto her two daughters in law, Go, return each to her mother's house: the LORD deal kindly with you, as ye have dealt with the dead, and with me.

The LORD grant you that ye may find rest, each of you in the house of her husband. Then she kissed them; and they lifted up their voice, and wept.

And they said unto her, Surely we will return with thee unto thy people.

And Naomi said, Turn again, my daughters: why will ye go with me? are there yet any more sons in my womb, that they may be your husbands?

Turn again, my daughters, go your way; for I am too old to have an husband. If I should say, I have hope, if I should have an husband also to night, and should also bear sons;

Would ye tarry for them till they were grown? would ye stay for them from having husbands? nay, my daughters; for it grieveth me much for your sakes that the hand of the LORD is gone out against me.

And they lifted up their voice, and wept again: and Orpah kissed her mother in law; but Ruth clave unto her.

And she said, Behold, thy sister in law is gone back unto her people, and unto her gods: return thou after thy sister in law.

And Ruth said, Intreat me not to leave thee, or to return from following after thee: for whither thou goest, I will go; and where thou lodgest, I will lodge: thy people shall be my people, and thy God my God:

Ruth 1:6-16

See Elisha and Elijah.

Do therefore according to thy wisdom, and let not his hoar head go down to the grave in peace.

I Kings 2:6

See Moses and Joshua.

See Barnabas and Saul.

But the Lord said unto him, Go thy way: for he is a chosen vessel unto me, to bear my name before the Gentiles, and kings, and the children of Israel: For I will shew him how great things he must suffer for my name's sake.

And Ananias went his way, and entered into the house; and putting his hands on him said, Brother Saul, the Lord, even Jesus, that appeared unto thee in the way as thou camest, hath sent me, that thou mightest receive thy sight, and be filled with the Holy Ghost.

But Barnabas took him, and brought him to the apostles, and declared
unto them how he had seen the Lord in the way, and that he had spoken to
him, and how he had preached boldly at Damascus in the name of Jesus.
And he was with them coming in and going out at Jerusalem.

Acts 9:15-17,27-28

We release to them the wisdom, direction, and vision that we've
obtained over the years. We could push them to their purpose. As
they validate and appreciate what God has done and is doing in us.
They don't have to start from scratch as we did. If we step up to the
challenge of mentorship, they could start from where we are. That's the
generational blessing that God desires to release; that each generation
could have an advantage that the previous one did not. Anytime we
have a pattern to refer to, we'll know better what God desires from
us, and more easily find and walk out our purpose. Beloved you have
so much, have learned so much, have lived so much; don't let another
generation miss out. We need, and I mean need, today's Elizabeth's
and Joseph's. Men and women of wisdom, instruction and God-
centered relationship that help others reach their destiny. That's what
helped Mary and that's what blessed Jesus throughout His life.

NEW SEASON - EXPANDING BY SERVING

Your age in numbers may count for AARP, but it doesn't discount
you from fulfilling your God-ordained destiny. By the way, you may
retire from civil service, but there is no retiring from kingdom service.
Serving is one of the reasons we are still living, and it's supposed to be
a way of living for each of us that profess Christ. Even if we are 50 or
60 plus, Jesus still expects our service. Abraham was still producing

something at 100, Moses was fulfilling destiny at 80, and Mordecai was still raising Godly babies well into his 60's; able to place a child into her God-given destiny that saved an entire nation. God still intends to use us in every area of ministry and He intends to get the glory. God is still looking for you to take the lead in responsibility and availability, and to support financially. Spiritually you have been positioned to help ministry move on to the next season. God is continuously writing your report of service to the Lord, its not over until He closes the eyes and mouth He has given us. If you've made it to this season of your life, obviously God desires for you to continue adding to and expanding the vision He's given you through your service. In every stage we experience we are to carry on enjoying the people and current time we are living in. If you are seasoned and single you really still have one priority.

> *But I would have you without carefulness. He that is unmarried careth for the things that belong to the Lord, how he may please the Lord:*
>
> *There is difference also between a wife and a virgin. The unmarried woman careth for the things of the Lord, that she may be holy both in body and in spirit: but she that is married careth for the things of the world, how she may please her husband.*
>
> 1 Corinthians 7:32,34

According to this text being unmarried is pleasing to our Lord. Plus your able to release those who are married and have young families from some of the stresses of ministry. If we focus on God's business, God will indeed focus on our business. I believe if you're not going to be found while waiting, but God causes you to be found

153

in service. This is not the season for shrinking or drawing back, but rather a time of serving.

I commend unto you Phebe our sister, which is a servant of the church which is at Cenchrea:

That ye receive her in the Lord, as becometh saints, and that ye assist her in whatsoever business she hath need of you: for she hath been a succourer of many, and of myself also.

Romans 16:1-2

She was a servant that made a difference, she caused substance to become evident. These people were themselves delivered and now able to support and aid the ministry for a greater scope of deliverance. Remember Mary Magdalene? She had seven demons bound inside her, but after all was said and done she had a lot of "Benjamins" and didn't mind supplying the needs of the Kingdom. Mary wasn't waiting to be married, she was working to make a difference and leaving behind a legacy of active ministry. They used all they had to bring the kingdom to pass.

Now it came to pass, as they went, that he entered into a certain village: and a certain woman named Martha received him into her house.

Luke 10:38

She had service at her house. Martha had the property. Mary had the money. Lazarus had the testimony. However, they all aided in bringing God the Glory. God is expecting these types of acts of service from all of us, regardless of age or stature,

154

Let not a widow be taken into the number under threescore years old, having been the wife of one man.

Well reported of for good works; if she have brought up children, if she have lodged strangers, if she have washed the saints' feet, if she have relieved the afflicted, if she have diligently followed every good work.

I Timothy 5:9-10

This is not about *retiring,* its all about *retooling.* We have to be flexible and understand that at the various stages of our lives we will have to re-evaluate our standing, but the goal to provide effective ministry always remains the same. Remember only what you do for Christ will last.

SEASON OF INTERCESSION

You will, during this season, have more control of your own time. There should be fewer distractions, not more of them. You are good and grown now. So now you should have more discipline resulting in greater times of intercession. The reality is that the cost of being free is always going to come with great responsibility. You may pray regularly but now with the extra time should come extra time in prayer. Now there is no one to stop you, no one to distract you or interrupt you. There are no kids coming home from school or any other hindrances so now should become an awesome season of prayer and worship. Truth is, the King and the kingdom are entrusting you with the grossly underestimated assignment of intercession. Your family, your ministry and those in spiritual authority over your life are banking on seasoned intercession from you. Prayer for the congregation, direction and for the vision to impact families and the city. It's at this point in your life that the everyday grind shouldn't be as demanding or time consuming. God expects us to be interceding, supplicating, covering and spiritually warring in prayer on behalf of the Kingdom's future. It's our intercession that causes blind eyes to opened, drug addicted to obtain freedom and strongholds to be torn down over the lives of people all over the world. For where the church is going and for where you are going, intercession is an absolute necessity. This is not just a woman thing, but it's a Christian thing specifically released to us for changing, delivering, shifting and for Kingdom advancing.

And, behold, there was a man in Jerusalem, whose name was Simeon; and the same man was just and devout, waiting for the consolation of Israel: and the Holy Ghost was upon him.

Luke 2:25

The Bible, time and time again, demonstrates the importance of those at this stage of life who took this stance.

Now she that is a widow indeed, and desolate, trusteth in God, and continueth in supplications and prayers night and day.

I Timothy 5:5

And there was one Anna, a prophetess, the daughter of Phanuel, of the tribe of Aser: she was of a great age, and had lived with an husband seven years from her virginity;

And she was a widow of about fourscore and four years, which departed not from the temple, but served God with fastings and prayers night and day.

Luke 2:36-37

In order for men and women to be great and effective in the Kingdom they had to first be great intercessors, then they were able to be great leaders. Abraham, Moses, Nehemiah, David etc. they were all great men of prayer. Truth be told, what we've been able to do in our lives is typically the result of prayer and usually what has been hindered in our lives is usually based on lack of prayer. Our financial status, marital status, emotional status and parental status has a lot to do with our prayer status.

And the prayer of faith shall save the sick, and the Lord shall raise him up; and if he have committed sins, they shall be forgiven him.

Confess your faults one to another, and pray one for another, that ye may be healed. The effectual fervent prayer of a righteous man availeth much.

James 5:15-16

Ask and it shall be

A lot of our receiving is tied to the level of our praying. Apparently, God wants you to be in a position without distraction to make Kingdom intercession. You have to guard your prayer life and time of intercession. Many times the enemy will try to divert you with various distractions (at times even relationships) as hindrances to you being in your place of intercession. If something causes you to abort intercession, watch out! If it forces you to miss fellowship, watch it! If it pulls you from discipleship, watch it! The enemy is trying knock you off of your path to purpose. Don't fall for it.

Let's take it a step further. Your intercession may not manifest only as a prayer warrior, one who is single and experienced to be in a position to intercede on behalf of others. You may well be the "Boaz" brother, a tested warrior, strong and able to intercede with financial support. You may be like a Joseph, favored and set in good position to be used at the appointed time for the Kingdom. You may be an Elizabeth, already blessed yourself yet you realize that what you've been through is for more than just you. If so, you must ask God to lead you to a Mary to minister to. By the way intercede for yourself as well. Stop waiting for everything to line up before you go out. Get a life; eat, shop, date or take your self out. Remember, Jesus' life was filled with intercession, but along with that, He lived His life; He traveled, fished, cruised, visited friends in different cities, and was even known to play with children. All of this was a form of intercession.

SEASON OF PERFECTING, PRODUCING AND POSSESSING

Keep in mind, this is still a time of growth and development. It is far more than a time of wandering, wavering, or daydreaming. It's actually a time of becoming, producing, reproducing and possessing. God gave the command for us to subdue, replenish and take dominion.

So God created man in his own image, in the image of God created he him; male and female created he them.

Genesis 1:27

So if we stop accomplishing these things it's not God it's us. God never commands us to do things that we are unable to carry out. Just because we are maturing, slowing, and maybe sometimes need a moment of rest doesn't mean we're ready to call it quits. This is not time for relaxing or gossiping.

And withal they learn to be idle, wandering about from house to house; and not only idle, but tattlers also and busybodies, speaking things which they ought not.

I Timothy 5:13

This not time to be a "busy body", rather we need to be busy completing Kingdom assignments and continuously chasing destiny. If we are not edifying, strengthening, or encouraging, then we need not to say anything at all. God doesn't want you to be found busy, but way outside of your lane. Busy work doesn't always translate into productive or efficient work. If you're caught up outside of destiny or with dealing things that don't quite pertain to His plan for you personally, then those things are stealing from your efficiency. God is not looking for folk who are "busy" in others lives and not living out our own. Those who are producing and flourishing in the House of the Lord are walking out their plan from God. They're drinking from "their cup" so to speak.

Those that be planted in the house of the LORD shall flourish in the courts of our God.

They shall still bring forth fruit in old age; they shall be fat and flourishing;

To shew that the LORD is upright: he is my rock, and there is no unrighteousness in him.

Psalm 92:13-15

Flourishing begins with a solid planting, constant watering, some purging and perfecting and then comes fruitful production. The "planting" refers to being a member planted in a local church.

Blessed is the man that walketh not in the counsel of the ungodly, nor standeth in the way of sinners, nor sitteth in the seat of the scornful.

But his delight is in the law of the LORD; and in his law doth he meditate day and night.

And he shall be like a tree planted by the rivers of water, that bringeth forth his fruit in his season; his leaf also shall not wither; and whatsoever he doeth shall prosper.

Psalm 1:1-3

If you are not spiritually planted you can't produce the way God intends you to produce. Where is your church? Where there is no planting there can be no producing. Where there is no watering there will be no growing. Where there is no purging there can be no maturation and where there is no maturation there will be no production of fruit.

But the fruit of the Spirit is love, joy, peace, longsuffering, gentleness, goodness, faith, Meekness, temperance: against such there is no law.

Galatians 5:22-23

As a matter of a fact, you, according to the Word, should be F.A.T. (**F**aithful, **A**vailable, & **T**eachable). You can still bring forth fruit in our old age. How fruitful are you? Where there is no fruit around there is usually no root found. You are called to, in this season, be F.A.T. and flourishing. You ought to be contributing something, increasing something, generating something or better yet possessing some things.

And now, behold, the LORD hath kept me alive, as he said, these forty and five years, even since the LORD spake this word unto Moses, while the children of Israel wandered in the wilderness: and now, lo, I am this day fourscore and five years old.

As yet I am as strong this day as I was in the day that Moses sent me: as my strength was then, even so is my strength now, for war, both to go out, and to come in.

Now therefore give me this mountain, whereof the LORD spake in that day; for thou heardest in that day how the Anakims were there, and that the cities were great and fenced: if so be the LORD will be with me, then I shall be able to drive them out, as the LORD said.

Joshua 14:10-12

Caleb at 80 maintained the agility, ability and faith to take a mountain full of giants. This is usually the time when some want to relax, however, this could be the time in life when you are being released in a greater measure. Recognize that there is still so much left to accomplish. This could be a time of big investing, advancing, conquering and bringing forth of all those old dreams and quiet hopes. Regardless of age, this should still be a time of doing and fulfilling the things we've forgotten or dropped along the way.

"Homework For the Plus Folk"

- Who could you be mentoring? (niece, daughter, neighbor, church sister, co-worker, classmate)
- Could you give one day a week for them? (lunch, shopping, movies, reading same book, prayer etc)

- Volunteer for prayer team, intercessory team at church.
- Become a prayer partner with someone in the congregation.
- Start a prayer group.
- Get a bucket list, then get started. (stuff you want to do before you die)
- Get a "Caleb List" of things you want to conquer in the future. (Driving, investing, sky diving, traveling, etc)
- In what areas would you like to become more fruitful?
- What's stopping you?
- What do you want to purchase or possess for you personally or as a gift of legacy?
- Review your retirement financial plan.
- Let someone in your family know your last wishes.
- Have you drawn up a will?

CHAPTER SEVEN: **SINGLE PLUS**

"Single parents are the 9th wonder of the world. For them there are no days off, only days on and with no off button."

~ *DBM*

CHAPTER EIGHT

SUCCESSFUL SINGLE PARENTING

While being a single parent is not God's original intent, He does however have a plan and a future for both you and your child or children

For I know the thoughts that I think toward you, saith the LORD, thoughts of peace, and not of evil, to give you an expected end.

Jeremiah 29:11

All through the holy scriptures God, who is the Author and Finisher of our faith, has calculated and counseled all things.

In whom also we have obtained an inheritance, being predestinated according to the purpose of him who worketh all things after the counsel of his own will:

Ephesians 1:11

This includes all of your things as well. Yes, He's got the money thing, the baby mama drama thing, back payment thing, and even the absentee father thing. The problem is not that you are now a single parent, but that you do not have a singleness of focus. Do you have singleness of purpose that pushes you to believe and to do what God has for you?

Behold, I and the children whom the LORD hath given me are for signs and for wonders in Israel from the LORD of hosts, which dwelleth in mount Zion.

Isaiah 8:18

Please, hear me when I say I'm not trying to condemn you my sister or my brother. After all, the book you hold in your hands is from a brother who comes from, by and through an awesome, faithful, strong and committed single mother. She is without a doubt, one of the major reasons why this kid from the projects is leading and serving in the Pastorate and blessed with a Doctorate. It is this experience that a large part of the reason I am so passionate about redeveloping the art of a committed family patriarch.

Sing, O heavens; and be joyful, O earth; and break forth into singing, O mountains: for the LORD hath comforted his people, and will have mercy upon his afflicted.

But Zion said, The LORD hath forsaken me, and my Lord hath forgotten me.

Can a woman forget her sucking child, that she should not have compassion on the son of her womb? yea, they may forget, yet will I not forget thee.

Behold, I have graven thee upon the palms of my hands; thy walls are continually before me.

Isaiah 49:13-16

Please, remember that one is a *whole number*. You are whole all by yourself, just you and Jesus. That being said, you should never accept anything or anyone less than that which would continue that wholeness in your life and in the life of those you're in covenant with. Don't instill into your children faulty family mentalities; they know mommy only really has two brothers (everyone you introduce them to cannot be their uncle) or that daddy only has so many female "friends". You know what I mean, don't act like you've never been there. We give them the wrong definitions and poor views of what could be and should be earnest, real and healthy family and social relationships.

Protect your children and your emotions by not running to introduce them to everyone you are seeing. This protects your children as well as yourself somewhat. My suggestion is that you impose a probation period of 60 to 90 days for an introduction to your children. Our families are a gift that must be earned, not put out front, but covered. Note, if you have a problem introducing them to your children at that point, you to take a long, hard, serious look at whether or not that individual is suitable. While I grew up thinking about what I was lacking tangibly, I never ever doubted the depth, weight and potency of my Mama loving me. Nor did I ever think we didn't have money. I realize now the value of some of those sacrifices that she made. She used to come to get me late at night after her second job, worn out on a regular basis, all the while still listening to my stories about all that transpired throughout my day. Checking to see if my homework was done, Ms. Clara Bell, my baby sitter, always made sure of that but she'd still check. Her not traveling, not going out partying or being in street doing what we affectionately called "hustling". As a matter of fact her being home was one of the best parts of my day, for that in it self was to me a success.

YOUR SUCCESS IS BASED ON KNOWING HOW GOD SEES YOU AND THEN ADJUSTING HOW YOU SEE YOU

And God said, Let us make man in our image, after our likeness: and let them have dominion over the fish of the sea, and over the fowl of the air, and over the cattle, and over all the earth, and over every creeping thing that creepeth upon the earth.

Genesis 1:26

While hindsight is good and insight is wonderful, the best way to see things is still by far seeing things through God's eyes. You have to stop looking at the current image of who you are and internalize the intended image of how God sees you from Genesis.

You've got to catch this; when we have missed it, blown it, or jacked it up, failed it, and repeated it, as long as we confess it and repent of it we are forgiven. We are, in God's eyes, put right back on track for purpose and destiny. You must realize that you are of great worth, and have expectation of great works in and through your life for God's Kingdom.

For we are his workmanship, created in Christ Jesus unto good works, which God hath before ordained that we should walk in them.

Ephesians 2:10

That was the true Light, which lighteth every man that cometh into the world.

John1:9

Know that your confession brings you freedom, and repentance demands that I produce fruit of a life that's headed in a different direction than before. Decisions don't define our person. They may lead to circumstances or conditions that skew our vision of who we are, but none of them change God's intent for our lives.

God is faithful, by whom ye were called unto the fellowship of his Son Jesus Christ our Lord.

1 Corinthians 1:9

Remember that you were a single person before you were a single parent. God doesn't change His expectation of you based on a natural birth. He defines you, calls you, empowers you, anoints you and plans to use you based on who you are by a spiritual birth

That which is born of the flesh is flesh; and that which is born of the Spirit is spirit.

John 3:6

There cometh a woman of Samaria to draw water: Jesus saith unto her, Give me to drink.

John 4:7

So even if you have been handled like Hagar, that doesn't define your future, nor does it illustrate God's view of you.

And Abraham rose up early in the morning, and took bread, and a bottle of water, and gave it unto Hagar, putting it on her shoulder, and the child, and sent her away: and she departed, and wandered in the wilderness of Beersheba. And the water was spent in the bottle, and she cast the child under one of the shrubs. And she went, and sat her down over against him a good way off, as it were a bow shot: for she said, Let me not see the death of the child. And she sat over against him, and lift up her voice, and wept.

And God heard the voice of the lad; and the angel of God called to Hagar out of heaven, and said unto her, What aileth thee, Hagar? fear not; for God hath heard the voice of the lad where he is. Arise, lift up the lad, and hold him in thine hand; for I will make him a great nation. And God opened her eyes, and she saw a well of water; and she went, and filled the bottle with water, and gave the lad drink. And God was with the lad; and he grew, and dwelt in the wilderness, and became an archer.

Genesis 21:14-20

You have to know that whether you face rejection, separation, lack of provision, jacked up relationships or seasons of isolation God still kept Hagar in His vision, stayed in communication with her, supplied provision and made of her a seed a nation! Know that like Hagar you being a single parent doesn't make God look at you any different. He already knew you'd be single and still expects His purpose for your life to shine through. Dare I say that God knew you would fall down, but He is banking on you choosing not to stay down. He is banking on you getting up, standing up and showing up at His appointed time for His intended purpose!

And the angel of the LORD found her by a fountain of water in the wilderness, by the fountain in the way to Shur.

Genesis16:7

The words "Angel of the Lord" mean Jehovah Nissi or "one who sees me and fights for me. My brother, my sister, you're not in this by yourself. See yourself worthy of being backed by Jesus, and whenever you mount up, He mounts up! When you fight He will fight! Hagar, you can handle this, besides, you have someone she didn't have in Christ Jesus! Here is my testimony. My mom worked two jobs for most of my childhood, and I was the second child. I never knew what second-hand clothes looked like. Somehow Jesus had seen her, provided for her and fought for her. You can and have to handle it like Hagar did.

And she called the name of the LORD that spake unto her, Thou God seest me: for she said, Have I also here looked after him that seeth me?

Genesis 16:13

And Sarah saw the son of Hagar the Egyptian, which she had born unto Abraham, mocking. Wherefore she said unto Abraham, Cast out this bondwoman and her son: for the son of this bondwoman shall not be heir with my son, even with Isaac. And the thing was very grievous in Abraham's sight because of his son. And God said unto Abraham, Let it not be grievous in thy sight because of the lad, and because of thy bondwoman; in all that Sarah hath said unto thee, hearken unto her voice; for in Isaac shall thy seed be called.

And also of the son of the bondwoman will I make a nation, because he is thy seed. And Abraham rose up early in the morning, and took bread, and a bottle of water, and gave it unto Hagar, putting it on her shoulder, and the child, and sent her away: and she departed, and wandered in the wilderness of Beersheba.

And the water was spent in the bottle, and she cast the child under one of the shrubs. And she went, and sat her down over against him a good way off, as it were a bow shot: for she said, Let me not see the death of the child. And she sat over against him, and lift up her voice, and wept.

And God heard the voice of the lad; and the angel of God called to Hagar out of heaven, and said unto her, What aileth thee, Hagar? fear not; for God hath heard the voice of the lad where he is.

Genesis 21:9-17

Now these are the generations of Ishmael, Abraham's son, whom Hagar the Egyptian, Sarah's handmaid, bare unto Abraham:

Genesis 25:12

Use what you've got, in this case it was sticks. God will use kingdom economics to make up the difference as it pertains to your expenses.

And they rose early in the morning, and went forth into the wilderness of Tekoa: and as they went forth, Jehoshaphat stood and said, Hear me, O Judah, and ye inhabitants of Jerusalem; Believe in the LORD your God, so shall ye be established; believe his prophets, so shall ye prosper.

And when he had consulted with the people, he appointed singers unto the LORD, and that should praise the beauty of holiness, as they went out before the army, and to say, Praise the LORD; for his mercy endureth for ever.

And when they began to sing and to praise, the LORD set ambushments against the children of Ammon, Moab, and mount Seir, which were come against Judah; and they were smitten.

For the children of Ammon and Moab stood up against the inhabitants of mount Seir, utterly to slay and destroy them: and when they had made an end of the inhabitants of Seir, every one helped to destroy another.

And when Judah came toward the watch tower in the wilderness, they looked unto the multitude, and, behold, they were dead bodies fallen to the earth, and none escaped.

And when Jehoshaphat and his people came to take away the spoil of them, they found among them in abundance both riches with the dead bodies, and precious jewels, which they stripped off for themselves, more than they could carry away: and they were three days in gathering of the spoil, it was so much.

II Chronicles 20:20-25

Your God has more stored in heaven than any man in any banking location anywhere on this earth. You've got to tap into your "offshore" provision. It's in the Kingdom. Kingdom sowing opens the bank of Kingdom favoring and Kingdom supply.

Bring ye all the tithes into the storehouse, that there may be meat in mine house, and prove me now herewith, saith the LORD of hosts, if I will not open you the windows of heaven, and pour you out a blessing, that there shall not be room enough to receive it.

And I will rebuke the devourer for your sakes, and he shall not destroy the fruits of your ground; neither shall your vine cast her fruit before the time in the field, saith the LORD of hosts.

And all nations shall call you blessed: for ye shall be a delightsome land, saith the LORD of hosts.

Malachi 3:10-12

Give, and it shall be given unto you; good measure, pressed down, and shaken together, and running over, shall men give into your bosom. For with the same measure that ye mete withal it shall be measured to you again.

Luke 6:38

SUCCESS COMES IN DEVELOPING A SUPPORT TEAM

And the things that thou hast heard of me among many witnessess, the same commit thou to faithful men, who shall be able to teach others also.

2 Timothy 2:2

When I refer to a support team I don't mean people that are just there in speculation and not in expectation. You need people with an actual hands on connection, relationship and with an awesome view of your child's future and purpose. If they cannot see your child the way you see your child, then they are not suited for your support team. This team should be made up of family, those who are living as examples, teachers who share your values, maybe even a neighbor. Not just any old neighbor, but one who believes in God and lives with Christ as their Lord and Savior. Ideally this would be an educator of some sort, one with dual vision both educational and parental. When possible, have some positive, God-loving, God-fearing men around in your life. They will show what it is to live committed, single and marital lives of integrity. This is key for boys to learn and emulate and important for girls in their future choices. What they are exposed to now will determine their frame of reference for later. Mama, grandma, a couple of good men (with proper motives), an educator and allowing them be around their father (given he is a loving, time-giving, spiritual living, relating father) and a mentor should make up the structure of this team.

Timothy's success was a direct result of this model. He had a grandma from his family (extended family who walk uprightly before God), the apostle Paul as an educator, mentor and one who lived out the example of a father. In other words, there was a support team in place to ensure he reached his full potential. He also had friends around him with same intentions, directions and convictions. Men of God with the same mind, heart and vision such as Titus. If we want godly success we should use God's process. Doesn't that make sense? All of these principles are intertwined to assist in getting a single parent the help they deserve and their child to their purpose.

When I call to remembrance the unfeigned faith that is in thee, which dwelt first in thy grandmother Lois, and thy mother Eunice; and I am persuaded that in thee also.

II Timothy 1:5

But continue thou in the things which thou hast learned and hast been assured of, knowing of whom thou hast learned them;

And that from a child thou hast known the holy scriptures, which are able to make thee wise unto salvation through faith which is in Christ Jesus.

II Timothy 3:14-15

But watch thou in all things, endure afflictions, do the work of an evangelist, make full proof of thy ministry.

II Timothy 4:5

SUCCESS COMES IN GETTING THEM INTO STRONG, STRUCTURED ENVIRONMENTS

Scripture to me is timeless, you ask the Holy Spirit and He will reveal answers to life's problems, situations and circumstances. He will guide you along by the Word and get you through the world and all it entails. One of the stories that helps me is the one about a family that goes through being broken and the separation of adoption, but in the end gets restored and repositioned. They all make it because they all actually operate in a structured manner. Everyone knew and played their position and all had the same affection and passion concerning one of the sons. You may have guessed it, it's the story of Moses.

Moses' mother loved him and was able to minister to him, but she also knew her limitations. She took him as far as she could and didn't give up or disown him, rather she situated him for a better outcome. His father who ends up having to step back and depend on God. He, his wife and daughter help his son reach, go after and live for the purpose that is on his life. In spite of the circumstances, he doesn't throw in the towel, instead he instructs and directs his boy, even if he has to do so from a position more removed than he'd have chosen. He trusts in God and looks toward the future, even if the process consists of his child not growing up in his own home. The sister who sees and understands the assignment on his life and doesn't hate him, but helps position him and set up the reconnection with his parents. Because of her posture, she was still able to have a healthy relationship with her brother.

Look how God can and will orchestrate His will in and through a complex, yet awesome structure. Everything about Moses' life was structured, his growing, learning, way of relating even his bathing had to be structured properly. This was not a form of lockdown, but all had to put down their desires and come into agreement for Moses' purpose being that they were all going to benefit ultimately anyway.

This can be handled today in the same way. First, let the situation rest on the water, the water of the word that is. Trust that God knows what He is doing even if you're struggling with it. It's imperative that you have a family member like the sister help watch him/her for you. This is not just watching naturally, but interceding and believing on their behalf. They must be in agreement with what God is doing. Like the father, it may appear as if he is doing nothing. The truth is that he is standing, believing and listening, looking without touching, yet never losing touch, as well as sharing instruction and direction. He is included in decisions, even if you're not living in his immediate area. Remember through it all, he is still caring for his wife and still tending to the other members of the family. Together with Pharaoh's daughter (someone in a privileged position) they partnered to raise one awesome leader.

I believe the secret was their commitment to work together and provide the appropriate structure. To the sister that is struggling with releasing your child to the other parents, a new home, a new school, to mentors, to new levels of relationships, new exposure and learning processes; if you handle it the right way, you too might get an invitation to be connected in that relationship and all benefit from it. It's all about being connected properly for the child's greater kingdom purpose.

At the end, remember what happened, he became both of their sons and the leader/deliverer of an entire nation. This helped me. I owe so much to my mother (Mom Cookie), Ms. Clara Bell, my adopted grandparents Mr. Lowell and Rose Mary Webb, or as we called them Mom-mom and Pop-pop. Oh, and especially to my Uncle Fred (Big Fred) and Aunt Sylvia, see they showed me that a family requires commitment and love and they were a living example that monogamy could be and should be a reality.

DON'T FORGET ABOUT THE BROTHERS

I realize that we focus on the strong, committed sisters who have been in this fight for what seems like forever. I respect and honor all the single parent mothers, but there are some men, who alone are handling the very same situation and dealing with those conditions. Believe it or not, they also know the frustration, isolation, rejection and anguish that ensues when doing your best to stay out of emotional confusion. This can be said for all parents, how much more for those filling dual family positions.

At the same time with the same mindset and God given passion, theirs is a valuable and incredible position in the kingdom. It doesn't matter how you got where you are whether it be by divorce, someone walked out, someone gave up, broke up or your predicament may even be due to a loss of life. I want you to know that God is using your situation for His purpose and for your good. Manhood is never defined simply by who we are in the physical realm, that's just called being male. Manhood in my humble opinion, begins when you begin to take responsibility for who you are and where you are, and when you stop blaming every other person for your current condition. Manhood is also accommodated by us making our decisions with the understanding that they are far reaching and will have a lasting impact and affect on others and not just ourselves. Manhood is a state that is defined by love, visible in our service and fulfilled by our commitment.

If you take a look at the men who raised their children and others' children, they all have those things in common. The Bible actually gives us a group of men that show what it is to be a single parent and make a kingdom difference:

Mordecai - This man never had his own children. His brother and his wife died and he was left with his niece. A little baby to care for with no wife, a little girl at that. Now you know he was busy. That's right, I'm referring to Esther. Their story is one of a single parent man in nothing short of an intriguing situation. Regardless of how he arrived there he was committed to stay there as a parent. He receives, restores, cultivates, raises, and eventually releases a woman called to rule one nation and deliver another one. You talk about a major assignment! He does all these things and does them well. She is able to accomplish all that God has called her to despite being raised by a single man,. She was led and trained by God and she completes her assignment without any manipulation. Mordecai taught her spiritually, raised her in purity, built her security, gave her identity, provided financially and positioned her for destiny. What an awesome single brother! There are others like the man and the minister Phillip, who raised four daughters while in kingdom service. Check out the results in Acts 21:8 –9. The evangelist Philip's greatest and most obvious legacy to me is the one he left with his family. They were four daughters that lived out humility, sexual purity and walked in a great prophetic anointing. My brother, God wants you to know that you can successfully raise your babies for God's glory,, and do so in a way that will leave an impact forever on our society!

JUST A WORD TO MY JOSEPH BROTHER'S (Men Struggling With Dating A Sister With Children)

Now the birth of Jesus Christ was on this wise: When as his mother Mary was espoused to Joseph, before they came together, she was found with child of the Holy Ghost.

Then Joseph her husband, being a just man, and not willing to make her a public example, was minded to put her away privily.

But while he thought on these things, behold, the angel of the LORD appeared unto him in a dream, saying, joseph, thou son of David, fear not to take unto thee Mary thy wife: for that which is conceived in her is of the Holy Ghost.

Matthew 1:18-20

When it comes to what we commonly call dating, it should be seen as God sees it. He connects people for purpose, fulfillment and representation. Somewhere in this process of dating you may come across a woman, a fine one, a wise one, a holy one, an incredible one and one that has a child or maybe even children. Instead of immediately thinking that you are not ready or prepared for a family, understand this, according to the word of God there is no family in the earth that has not been prepared, preplanned or prescheduled by the incomprehensible wisdom of God.

In whom also we have obtained an inheritance, being predestinated according to the purpose of him who worketh all things after the counsel of his own will:

Ephesians 1:11

This may be your Joseph moment.

But while he thought on these things, behold, the angel of the LORD appeared unto him in a dream, saying, Joseph, thou son of David, fear not to take unto thee Mary thy wife: for that which is conceived in her is of the Holy Ghost.

Matthew 1:20

The reality is that God wants you to do something far greater than just satisfy yourself. He may be giving you an opportunity to be a key part of a greater assignment or maybe even greater kingdom glory.

Now the birth of Jesus Christ was on this wise: When as his mother Mary was espoused to Joseph, before they came together, she was found with child of the Holy Ghost.

Matthew 1:18

Your concern may be how or where they fit into my destiny. Consider this, if Joseph misses out on this, he misses out on seeing

Jesus, that alone should settle it in your heart. If you choose to discard it without seeking God's heart, you could miss out on one of the greatest places of purpose known to any of us. Oh yes, and maybe, quite possibility it could be the work of or all have been orchestrated by the Holy Ghost. Listen Joseph, you could be missing the love of your life, and possibly the one your God intended to be your wife. Listen, if she already has a child or children, she definitely doesn't need another one, so if you are not Joseph don't hinder her or the children in their God-intended process or purpose with any foolishness. Don't let your own selfishness, self-centeredness or earthly ideal of success make you pass on one of life's greatest purposes. What's that you may ask, it's this process and relationship where you get be like Jesus in a sense. Hear me out, you see he is the one who accepted us.

To the praise of the glory of his grace, wherein he hath made us accepted in the beloved.

Ephesians 1:6

He is the one who showed unconditional love by adopting us.

Having predestinated us unto the adoption of children by Jesus Christ to himself, according to the good pleasure of his will,

Ephesians 1:5

Yes, He adopted us into His body and into God's kingdom family. Lest we forget, God used Him to save us and deliver us while the church was not, nor are we now perfect or spotless. We all benefit from the forgiveness and unconditional love of Christ Jesus. Through Him we have all become God's children. In this love and in time, the ones that were called hers become the ones called yours or ours, just like God, "a people that were not my people have become my people."

"Homework For Potential Joseph's"
Consider these things:

- Could you be missing God?
- Could you miss the love of your life?
- Don't let selfishness make you pass up one of life's greatest purposes.
- You could get to do for Jesus, what Jesus did for us!
- Am I open for change at God's choosing?
- Does public opinion overrule God's intentions?
- Is it about you or them?
- Does your life have room for more than just your life?
- If it's God's decision am I willing to obey?
- Am I that selfish that I just don't want to share my life?
- Is it about the guys or the one God led me to find?
- We were not His people, but have been made His through redemption.

THE MINISTRY CALLED FAMILY

ABOUT THE AUTHOR

DR. DAVID B. MILLS

***Dr. David B. Mills**, Founder and Senior Pastor of Through The Word Bible Fellowship, located in Chester, PA. He has been married for 17 years to his childhood sweetheart, Bernadette, who partners with him in ministry and they have five children.*

Dr. David B. Mills was licensed and ordained in 1991. Dr. David B. Mills served in the Navy for five years and has translated that experience to the church where order, structure and discipline are a significant part of the emphasis. He has also had the privilege to travel to several continents as a result of his navy experience such as Asia, throughout North America and the Middle East where he was stationed for 181 days. As a result, he believes this has attributed to him being a strong supporter of world missions and believes that the church is obligated to sow there if they are not able to go there.

Dr. David B. Mills has attended Christian Research and Development, Philadelphia, PA, under the auspices of Dr. Willie Richardson. While there he received his Certification For Biblical Counseling, and completed the coursework for "Pastoring With A Purpose." He has also completed coursework at Center For Urban Theological Studies. Dr. David B. Mills recently received his Doctorate Degree from Minnesota Graduate School of Theology, August 2006. In August of 2008, Dr. David B. Mills completed Kingdom University, Atlanta, GA, under the auspices of Dr. Cindy N Trimm.

Dr. David B. Mills has had the privilege to be a guest several times this year on "TBN" to teach on "The Family" as well as "Marriage and Ministry". He is sought after to minister at Leadership, Marriage, Men, Women & Youth conferences throughout the country. He has attended many conferences and seminars for personal growth and development such as: John Maxwell's Catalyst Conference, Rick Warrens' Purpose Driven Life, Dr. IV Hilliard's Church Growth; T.D. Jakes Pastor's Conference; and annually he attends Living Waters International Alliance Leadership Conference, hosted by his Overseer, Bishop Steven W. Banks, Newport News, VA.

Made in the USA
Charleston, SC
17 March 2013